More praise for *Leading Congregations through Crisis*

"The knowledge and experiences Greg shares in this book, although written specifically for congregations, can also be applied in situations with any Christian organization."

Linda C. Fuller, Co-founder of Habitat for Humanity International and the Fuller Center for Housing

LEADING CONGREGATIONS
THROUGH CRISIS

GREGORY L. HUNT

CHALICE PRESS

ST. LOUIS, MISSOURI

Bible quotations, unless otherwise noted, are from the *New Revised Standard Version Bible*, copyright 1989, Division of Christian Education of the National Council of the Churches of Christ in the United States of America. Used by permission. All rights reserved.

Scripture quotations marked (TLB) are taken from *The Living Bible*, copyright © 1971. Used by permission of Tyndale House Publishers, Inc., Wheaton, Illinois 60189. All rights reserved.

Cover and interior design: Scribe Inc.

www.chalicepress.com

10 9 8 7 6 5 4 3 2 1   12   13   14   15   16   17

PRINT: 9780827221703   EPUB: 9780827221710   EPDF: 9780827221727

Library of Congress Cataloging-in-Publication Data

Hunt, Gregory Lynn, 1954–
Leading congregations through crisis / by Gregory Hunt.
    p. cm.
Includes bibliographical references and index.
   ISBN 978-0-8272-2170-3 (alk. paper)
   1. Tragic, The–Religious aspects–Christianity. 2. Crisis management–Religious aspects–Christianity. 3. Christian leadership. 4. Pastoral counseling. I. Title.
BR115.T73H86 2012
   253–dc23   2012010758

Contents

Editor's Foreword

Inspiration and Wisdom for Twenty-First-Century
Christian Leaders

You have chosen wisely in deciding to study and learn from a book published in The Columbia Partnership Leadership Series with Chalice Press. We publish for

- Congregational leaders who desire to serve with greater faithfulness, effectiveness, and innovation.
- Christian ministers who seek to pursue and sustain excellence in ministry service.
- Members of congregations who desire to reach their full kingdom potential.
- Christian leaders who desire to use a coach approach in their ministry.
- Denominational and parachurch leaders who want to come alongside affiliated congregations in a servant leadership role.
- Consultants and coaches who desire to increase their learning concerning the congregations and Christian leaders they serve.

The Columbia Partnership Leadership Series is an inspiration- and wisdom-sharing vehicle of The Columbia Partnership, a community of Christian leaders who are seeking to transform the capacity of the North American church to pursue and sustain vital Christ-centered ministry. You can connect with us at www.TheColumbiaPartnership.org.

Primarily serving congregations, denominations, educational institutions, leadership development programs, and parachurch organizations, the Partnership also seeks to connect with individuals, businesses, and other organizations seeking a Christ-centered spiritual focus.

We welcome your comments on these books, and we welcome your suggestions for new subject areas and authors we ought to consider.

The Columbia Partnership
332 Valley Springs Road, Columbia, SC 29223-6934
Voice: 803.622.0923, www.TheColumbiaPartnership.org

Foreword

What are you going to do when your congregation experiences an unexpected interruption? A crisis. It is not "if." It is "when." Do you have a crisis response plan? A crisis prevention plan? (As if you could prevent an unexpected interruption.)

My friend Floyd Craig, a religious organization communication consultant, has always said that the foolish among us do not have a crisis response plan. The wise among us have one, but know it will never work exactly as the plan calls for when a crisis occurs. It is certainly going to take a whole bunch of prayer and action. It is going to take wisdom that can ultimately come only from our God, who sees the future and the consequences of our actions.

The Situation

On July 12, 2009, I was deacon of the week for my church in Columbia, South Carolina. I attended both morning worship services, enjoyed lunch out with my wife, and upon returning home for the afternoon I turned on my computer to check my e-mail and social networks. Soon I began to see notices of a bus accident involving a youth group and sponsors from First Baptist Church of Shreveport, Louisiana, where my friend Greg Hunt was pastor. It was surreal.

Later I had several contacts with Greg about the situation. I had been engaged by the church a couple of years earlier to consult with them concerning their future. Many of the people impacted by the tragedy Greg describes in this book were people I had met. Eventually Greg and I began to talk about how unfortunate it is that although multiple congregations go through crises like this, seldom are they fully prepared, if it is possible to be prepared.

Further, what happens after a crisis of this nature, and many other types of crises, is crucial to the long-term spiritual and emotional health of the congregational community and many individuals and households connected with the congregation. The six to eighteen months after a crisis are times for essential relief, recovery, and renewal actions. Without healthy responses many people and congregations can be dysfunctional for a lifetime.

The Long-Term Response

This book contains what Greg and I began to talk about a few months following the bus accident. We identified possible types of crises. We conducted a survey to discover the types of crises most frequently experienced by congregations throughout North America. We identified more than a hundred case studies for consideration. From this list Greg discerned those situations that would fit in a book about leading congregations through a crisis. I am pleased that a person who has spent several decades in pastoral ministry and has also had a focus on healthy marriages and families, could craft this exceptional book.

We cannot ignore these crises. Their memory will not go away. Their impact is felt for a long time. It takes endings, transitions, and new beginnings to work through them. In my consulting work I am often reminded of the crises congregations face, and how they respond well or badly.

I Cannot Get It out of My Mind!

Recently I was thinking about unusual crises congregations face. Here are ten that came to mind:

Number Ten: A tornado comes through a small town, right down Main Street, and fully or significantly destroys all five church buildings in the downtown area. This is a major disruption in the life of all the congregations and becomes the occasion for many other issues of concern in the congregations to rise to the surface. Within a year not only are none of the five pastors still serving these congregations, but none of them are in Christian ministry.

Number Nine: The former pastor of your church is now the pastor of a church in another state. His wife calls you up one day because the two of you are still best friends, and exclaims, "Vickie, our church is on fire!" You reply, "Michele, that is wonderful! It is great to be part of a church that is really on fire for the . . ." "Shut up, Vickie", Michele interrupts. "Our church is on fire and it is burning to the ground!"

Number Eight: The economic recession throughout the world has impacted a congregation to the point that the church must downsize staff. Every staff person has a support group of people in the congregation who declare, "Not my staff person!" The church makes the tough decisions, and all heaven breaks loose. (Or was it another word?)

Number Seven: For some reason the pastor quits preaching in the middle of his sermon. He calls for the congregation to sing the hymn of commitment. He stops the singing after one verse, pronounces the benediction, turns around, and goes to his office crying uncontrollably. Two days later he leaves town for seven weeks, goes to his place of birth, and tries to figure out what is going on with him. It is difficult for the congregation to watch him burn out right in front of them. Many people begin thinking about their own life situation.

Number Six: The remnants of a major hurricane come through a community, and flash floods begin occurring on Sunday morning while the congregation is at worship. As people start to leave, they find that emergency vehicles are blocking the roads around town in low-lying areas.

Many people cannot get home, and multiple people—including the pastor's family—lose their homes to the floods. Even the church experiences major damage and is unusable for six months. A significant number of families never return to regular worship at the church.

Number Five: A youth minister who once served your church is arrested for inappropriate sexual contact with several teenage girls in his current church. Families question their daughters about inappropriate approaches from this former youth minister, and a spirit of distrust escalates when it is discovered the same thing happened in your church. This comes on the heels of similar accusations about a layman who was the leader of teenage boys in a neighboring church.

Number Four: A new church secretary suspects something about the finances she is required to handle and reports this to the pastor. An audit shows that more than $86,000 is missing from various church accounts over a three-year period. Evidence points to the former secretary, yet a church committee had supposedly audited those financial records annually.

Number Three: After years of study and debate, your denomination decides to affirm the ordination of gays and lesbians as clergy persons. Your congregation has always said that it would leave the denomination if and when this happened. Yet it still takes your congregation more than a year to decide to leave, and you lose 20 percent of the membership during that year as people move to other congregations in protest of the denominational decision. When your congregation leaves, the denomination's financial agency executes a clause in the mortgage they hold on your property that calls for the note to immediately be due in full.

Number Two: Three people are killed in a shooting at the high school a block away from your church. One is a teenager from your church. Two others from your church are wounded. The shooter is a teenager who has been to some of your youth meetings and tried to get a certain girl to date him, but she rejected him. She is the teenager from your church who has been killed.

Number One: A three-year-old boy in your church weekday preschool falls off a swing on your church playground when the swing breaks, and he has severe head trauma that requires long-term rehabilitation. The one preschool teacher on the playground at the time had left the area to chase a ball another child had thrown over the fence. The family of the three-year-old boy sues the church, the maker of the equipment, and the installer, who is also a member of the church. Five or six families pull their children out of the preschool program.

Your Response?

On a sheet of paper, your computer, or your digital tablet write down the first five ideas that come to mind as crises that are most likely to happen in your congregation. Next write down the five crises that you think are least likely to happen in your congregation because "they just could not happen here."

Next ask yourself if your congregation has a crisis response plan. If one of the crises you have recorded were to happen in your congregation, do you have a plan in place as to what needs to happen, who needs to do it, how communication will be handled, and who will be the authorized spokesperson for your congregation? What will be your spiritual response to any of these crises, and who will lead it? What will be your legal response or shield for any of these crises, and who is the attorney who will handle it for you? Do you have appropriate and adequate insurance to cover unexpected crises?

If your congregation does not have a crisis response plan, how soon can you develop one? Who will do it? What outside resource information or persons do you need to help you develop this plan? While certainly the Triune God will be present with your congregation during crises, it is irresponsible not to do everything that is reasonable and feasible to anticipate crises and protect the church.

Developing a plan is all about what to do when crises happen. Is there another way to look at this?

Crisis Prevention

In addition to having a crisis response plan, every congregation needs to engage in risk management activities. Some crises are preventable. Others are not; they just happen. But has your church undergone a risk management study of the church facilities, and the church policies and procedures, to be sure the congregation has taken reasonable and customary steps to lower risk and liability?

Move Forward

With this background, move forward to read this book. Ponder your ministry setting as a pastor, staff person, or lay leader. What will your congregation do to prepare for and to respond to the next crisis it faces?

George Bullard
Strategic Coordinator, The Columbia Partnership at
www.TheColumbiaPartnership.org
General Secretary, North American Baptist Fellowship of
the Baptist World Alliance
www.NABF.info

Introduction

This is the book I wish I had had years ago. I readily confess that when dealing with congregational crises in the past, I and the leaders with whom I collaborated did a good bit of improvisation. Without a sourcebook such as this one, we had little to go by except our faith, character, experience, and imagination. We fashioned our responses on the fly and hoped for the best. Having put the crises behind us, we seldom took time to record our experiences, evaluate what worked and didn't, or harvest lessons for the future. We had a general sense of how God had used the experience to refine us, but mostly we thanked God for the gift of resilience and moved on. We counted on our collective memory to guide us the next time around.

Now we know a better way. No two congregational crises are exactly alike, but they all share important characteristics and so lend themselves to leadership practices that transfer well from one context to another. We can learn from the successes and failures of other congregational leaders.

Crisis leadership and management have become subjects of special interest, especially in the worlds of business, education, government, and the military. Crisis management has become a science as well as an art. Any corporation, school, government agency, or regiment worth its salt has a plan for avoiding avoidable crises and responding effectively to the crises that come—even unexpected ones.

Taking a cue from these worlds, church-related organizations have developed a wide array of resources to prevent, prepare for, and resolve congregational crises. This rich body of material helps church leaders take the mystery out of crisis leadership and management. We have every reason to take full advantage of the lessons leaders are learning wherever crisis-related issues come into play.

What Brings You to This Book?

A variety of situations may have brought you to this book. You may be a crisis-seasoned leader who wants a handy reference guide to remind you of lessons you've learned the hard way. You may be new to crisis leadership and wise enough to know you need help. You may be leading a congregation through crisis right now. You may have picked up this book not out of a general interest in the topic, but because you want immediate guidance for getting your church through difficult straits. You may belong to a group of leaders who are using this book to develop collaborative crisis plans.

This book has been designed with all these possibilities in mind. It will prepare you to lead more effectively through future crises, if, at the present moment, everything's rocking along nicely. It will serve you right now, if the congregation you serve finds itself navigating the treacherous waters of trouble. This book will

- highlight key principles for leading through crisis
- share stories from church and culture that bring these principles to life
- provide opportunities for you to reflect on these principles as they come into play in your circumstances as a leader

Crisis Leadership as a Team Activity

Let me encourage you to include others in the study of this book. As will become apparent, crisis leadership is a team activity. No one should go it alone.

For Those Who Aren't Dealing with a Crisis Now. If you haven't already, let me encourage you to identify four to eight key leaders who will work through this book together. It may be a preexisting leadership group or an ad hoc group, depending on your church's current structure and circumstances. Make copies of the book available for each group member. Decide together on the pace at which you will read it and reflect on it. Use the questions at the end of each chapter as starting points for personal reflection. Agree on times to meet as a group and discuss your insights. Use your times together to learn from one another and develop consensus about follow-up action steps you will take to better prepare your congregation for crises.

For Those in the Throes of Crisis Now. Hopefully, you have a team of leaders participating in crisis response. If not, I strongly encourage you to gather other leaders around you as soon as you can. Chapters 4 and 5 include insight into the selection and work of this team. Get a copy of this book into the hands of fellow leaders, encouraging them to read through the book. Schedule a leadership gathering to discuss the book, answering the following questions:

- Based on the information in this book, what have we done well?
- What have we not yet done that we need to do—immediately? In the near future? Sometime?
- What insights from the book stand out as particularly important for us, given our situation?
- What insights beyond this book have come to us during the course of our reading?

You don't have to create a leadership recipe from scratch. The accumulated wisdom of leaders across time can be distilled into key principles. You can build on these principles as you customize your congregation's response. Your congregation can deal with whatever happens and grow stronger as a result. That's the prayer for you that has guided me every step of the way in the creation of this book.

PART I

The Anatomy of Congregational Leadership in a Time of Crisis

1

One Minister's Tales of Crisis

Crisis can strike when you least expect it.

At 10:20 a.m., on Sunday, July 12, 2009, a busload of twenty-three youth and adult sponsors from the church I was pastoring—First Baptist Church, Shreveport, Louisiana—headed east on Interstate 20, on the way to a missions-oriented camp in Macon, Georgia. They passed Meridian, Mississippi, making good time toward their destination.

Suddenly one of the two left rear tires blew out, causing the bus to swerve and then flip three times before landing on its side on the shoulder of the highway. Everyone on board got tossed out of their seats, some were thrown through windows, and two ended up trapped under the bus. A few lucky ones got out of the bus with nothing more than bruises and abrasions. Several suffered serious injuries. A bright fifteen-year-old boy, Brandon Ugarte, died at the scene.

Back in Shreveport, we were moments away from beginning our two 10:30 a.m. worship services when word of the accident reached us. One of the adults on the trip—a First Baptist Church staff person—called his wife from the crash scene. In a panic, she came to me with the news. All we knew at our end was that our bus had flipped. Our initial impression was that there were injuries, but none were life-threatening.

We worshiped in a high state of alarm that morning, praying earnestly and hoping for the best. We soon learned just how serious the accident had been. The tragedy thrust us into a state of crisis, calling for leadership under extreme conditions. I and other congregational leaders pooled our wisdom to meet the challenge. I drew on every lesson I had ever learned over the course of decades of pastoral ministry. It wasn't the first time crisis had struck a congregation I led.

Conflict and Crisis

My earliest brush with congregational crisis occurred in my first professional assignment. First Baptist Church, Knoxville, Tennessee, had called me to a one-year seminarian internship as college minister. Soon after my arrival, members of the church came to blows with their relatively new senior pastor over the Saturday-night firing of the long-tenured minister of music. As a bystander for the most part, I watched the stages of crisis unfold. Initial shock led to anger. Then leaders stepped in with damage control and conflict resolution.

I took note of the ripple effects of the crisis when the senior pastor subsequently hired a minister of music with whom he had worked elsewhere. I took further note of the lingering consequences when that minister of music, after only a few months on the job, resigned abruptly and returned to the church from which he had come. It wasn't a pretty picture, with as many lessons about how *not* to handle things as how to get it right.

Disease and Death in Rural Kentucky

The very next year and while still a seminarian, I became pastor of a small, rural church in a town of 385 in north central Kentucky. During my three years of ministry there, the community seemed to exist in a perpetual state of crisis. The most dramatic occurrence involved disease and death. Debbie, a twenty-year-old wife and new mother, contracted a lethal bacterial disease, meningococcemia. She died at a nearby hospital within hours of the first signs of illness, leaving behind her one-month-old daughter, Tasha, and her nineteen-year-old husband, Wayne.

Three months later, Tasha, now four months old, contracted the same bacterial disease and died as quickly as her mom had, despite being transported to an excellent hospital in Cincinnati. As if that weren't enough, three other children who were close to the family, including our own daughter, developed similar symptoms the same day, raising horrifying fears among families and grave concern among health officials that we were dealing with a grim epidemic.

In a crazy quirk of timing, doctors determined that our daughter and one other child had nothing more than stomach viruses. The fourth symptomatic child had a mild case of viral meningitis. Adding to this tragedy and trauma, Wayne, while his daughter lay dying, got news that his eighteen-year-old brother had been killed in a car accident while playing "chicken" with a friend on the highway outside of town.

At the age of twenty-six I got a crash course in caring for traumatized families, shepherding a terrified church, and partnering with public officials to manage a community crisis. I also got a bittersweet taste of the impact of a congregational crisis on a leader. It felt gratifying to care for those affected and to help restore sanity to the panicked community, but our daughter's involvement in the crisis added a layer of trauma to the grief I already felt for people I had grown to love. I had an up-close-and-personal experience with compassion fatigue as the urgent care of the early days turned into weeks and months of dealing with the lingering effects of what had taken place.

A Staff Problem Becomes a Church-Wide Crisis

Three years later, now pastoring another church and working toward the completion of my Ph.D., crisis struck again. This time the crisis involved a conflict with a staff member that spilled into the church. Before the crisis was over, the church had divided into camps, the staff member had been fired, and I—exhausted and disheartened by the process—had decided to resign. I learned some hard lessons about handling personnel matters, working through lay leadership, and managing stress. I walked away from the experience wondering if I would finish my degree or pastor again. I continued to call on the lessons of this experience in the years following as I led other churches through disagreements over personnel as well as over such things as denominational affiliation and ministry direction.

Budget Woes

I did finish my degree and served many years in congregational ministry. In 1989, after four years as an associate pastor, I became the senior pastor of Holmeswood Baptist Church in Kansas City, Missouri. This proved to be one of my most satisfying and fruitful experiences in ministry. That does not mean the church avoided crisis.

The church had a long history of financial and ministry health. Seven years into my ministry, Holmeswood ran a standard fall stewardship campaign. Unexpectedly, this one ended poorly, raising the specter of severe budget cuts, difficult staff reductions, and serious ministry disruption. Rather than succumb to cutback fever, I challenged church leaders to consider strategies for strengthening member giving. Together we prayed and led the church in a two-month experience of congregational reflection and renewal. The financial crisis became a transformative moment in the life of the church, leading to renewed vision and passion and a $220,000 financial turnaround.

Mother Nature Strikes

In 2003, I accepted the call to return as senior pastor of the church I had served as associate pastor after my seminary days: First Baptist Church, Shreveport, Louisiana. I had no way of knowing how situational crisis would impact our lives together.

In late August 2005, Hurricane Katrina struck the Gulf coast and left New Orleans and other communities in southern Louisiana devastated. This natural disaster created a major regional crisis and put unprecedented pressure on the church and community to respond. An estimated sixty thousand evacuees ended up on the doorstep of Shreveport-Bossier City in northwest Louisiana, prompting a tidal wave of community-wide collaboration. Our church stayed in the middle of the action, providing shelter, supplies, volunteer service, and long-term care. We also extended our efforts with recovery expeditions to southern Louisiana and pace-setting involvement in a new housing initiative in Shreveport in partnership with the Fuller Center for Housing.

Tragedy on the Highway

I put lessons from all these earlier crises into play when leading First Baptist through the early stages of its recovery from the highway tragedy. I say "the early stages" because six weeks before the accident, I had announced plans to transition out of pastoral leadership and devote myself full-time to Directions, Inc., a nonprofit organization my wife and I had formed in 2001.[1] After careful deliberation, other key leaders and I agreed to stick with plans for an August 31 departure. We made the most of my last weeks there, setting things in motion that would serve the congregation for months to come. I devoted my last days at First Baptist to crisis response.

Facilitating congregational recovery involved several things: bringing together a crisis management team, encouraging the faith and hope of the congregation, and helping to channel the congregation's love into meaningful short-term and long-term action. As we dealt with the inevitable challenges of the aftermath, we also managed unprecedented media attention. What began with the intense interest of local media quickly became a steady stream of interest from national media. Though I served as the principal interface between the church and the media, I had outstanding support from news-related veterans in the congregation.

Faithful leaders and servants in the church, with valuable support from skilled professionals and generous-hearted congregations in the region, responded to our crisis with wise, timely, and compassionate care. The crisis brought out the best in us as a church, enlivening our worship, our prayer, and our self-giving spirit.

None of this could erase the impact of the accident. We joined the Ugarte family as they grieved for their son. Three weeks later, twelve-year-old Maggie Lee Henson, the daughter of our associate pastor, lost her battle for life. Our prayers for her recovery became prayers for God's mercy toward her mom, dad, and younger brother.

Others suffered acute injuries that would take months to heal. We set plans in motion to support them every step of the way. Everyone involved in the accident—those on the bus, their families, and their principal caregivers—bore emotional wounds from the experience. We anticipated their needs with a "post-critical-incident" strategy that drew on the expertise of mental health professionals.

The ripple effects of the bus accident continued for months. Families and friends grieved two untimely deaths. Others rehabbed from injuries and surgeries. Legal questions relating to liability and medical bills had to be resolved. As for congregational learning and development, the church revisited its policies and procedures for church-sponsored road trips and further refined what were already very responsible safeguards.

From my ongoing contact with those who remained in leadership after my departure, I have been impressed by First Baptist's ability to build on the healing that occurred during my final weeks as pastor. They still have issues to deal with, but the cloud of crisis has lifted and the missional spirit of the congregation lives on.

A Career of Lessons Learned

As this chapter makes clear, I came by my interest in the topic of this book naturally. All my experiences with congregational crisis, culminating with First Baptist Shreveport's brave and loving response to a bus accident, have heightened my appreciation for the importance of leading well when crises come.

Combined, these stories suggest several of the ways crises can strike. They introduce themes that come into play as leaders lead their congregations through crisis. Anyone who has led for long at the congregational level has personal stories to tell. Most, if not all, would agree that

- congregational crises are inevitable,
- they come in many shapes and sizes,
- they represent a serious threat to the church and everyone involved,
- how the church responds in the short run makes a big difference in the long run,
- effective crisis leadership is essential.

Reflection Questions

Reflect personally on the following questions. If you are using this book in a group study, share your perspectives with each other.

- What experiences have you had with congregational crisis?
- What leadership lessons have you learned from those experiences?

2

Understanding
Congregational Crisis

Stressful things happen on any given week in a congregation's life. A beloved member ends up in the hospital. Bad weather negatively affects participation in a ministry or program. Tough decisions have to be made at a finance committee meeting. People come into conflict with each other over worship style or the color of the paint.

Stressful situations can strike at any moment. They echo the far-reaching truth psychiatrist Scott Peck teaches us: "Life is difficult."[1] Accepting that life is difficult spares us the extra layer of self-induced stress. We add this stress to situations because we hate complications. Accepting this in congregational life frees us to get on with problem solving in pursuit of our congregation's God-given mission.

New complications invade congregational life every week, which is only normal. Sometimes, however, the complications go beyond what's normal. They crash in on us unexpectedly and disrupt everything else that's going on. They divert our attention and demand our full and immediate attention. When this happens, we're dealing with a crisis.

Let's take a closer look at what we're talking about when it comes to congregational crisis, get a handle on key terms, and take a preliminary look at the kinds of crises that can disrupt our lives together.

The Vocabulary of Crisis

Let's begin with a glossary of key terms related to crisis.

Critical incident. A critical incident is *a dramatic, destabilizing development that presents apparent danger and uncertainty.* The incident or development itself is not a crisis, but it carries with it the real potential to provoke a crisis response. Consider, for instance, a factory shutdown. The shutdown qualifies as a critical incident; but those working at the factory will experience the shutdown in a variety of ways that will depend on such things as their level of financial security and the availability of alternate work. Full-time workers who live from paycheck to paycheck and who have no other job prospects will react differently than those who aren't dependent on their income from the factory or who have readily available employment options. Those whose livelihoods depend on the factory job will likely experience the shutdown as a crisis.

A critical incident triggers a rapid-fire internal assessment process. We ask ourselves: Does this incident pose a serious threat either physically, emotionally, relationally, cognitively, or spiritually? Assuming that our answer is *yes*, the next question would be, can this threat be resolved readily using available resources and coping strategies? Problems that lend themselves to convenient solutions or that lie within the scope of our current level of competence and confidence are not likely to provoke a crisis. We say we're in crisis when the threat gets the best of us and thrusts us beyond our perceived ability to cope.[2]

Crisis. A crisis, then, is not the precipitating event, though we sometimes use the term this way in casual conversation. Technically, a crisis is what those who specialize in crisis intervention call "a response condition."[3] Three things characterize this condition: (1) we're caught off-balance, (2) our usual coping mechanisms don't prove a match for the problems as we perceive them, and (3) we experience high-level distress that impairs our normal functioning.

The term *crisis* means "a turning point for better or worse." It comes from the Greek word, *krisis*, which literally means "decision."[4] A crisis puts us at a crossroad where decisions must be made—under pressure—that will impact the course of our lives, positively or negatively, from that moment forward.

The decisions we make don't, by themselves, guarantee the outcome of a crisis. Factors beyond our control continue to influence developments. Consider the crisis point in a serious illness, for instance. As we wait for a loved one's fever to break, we know that dynamics beyond our doing will spell the outcome.

Crisis, by its very nature, confronts us with our vulnerabilities and limitations. Even if we have played a part in prompting the developments, in crisis we experience unintended consequences that leave us scrambling to get a handle on the situation.

Emergencies and disasters. Emergencies and disasters are particular kinds of critical incidents. In an *emergency*, unforeseen circumstances create a need for urgent response. This can occur on any scale, from a bump on the head that calls for an ice pack to a stock market free fall that triggers global reactions. We reserve the term *disaster* for large-scale emergencies, or "sudden calamitous event[s] bringing great damage, loss, or destruction."

Some emergencies don't precipitate a crisis. I remember, for instance, the night my wife, Priscilla, went into labor with our first child three weeks before the due date. We had prepared for months for this moment, though we didn't anticipate it coming so soon. Nevertheless, we knew where to go and basically what to expect. We felt very calm as we gathered up our prepacked bags and headed to the hospital. We even stopped on the way to get cash from an ATM. I jokingly expressed disappointment to Priscilla that we didn't have an excuse for speeding.

Other emergencies do precipitate a crisis. First Baptist Shreveport's bus accident was as an emergency that sent everyone involved into immediate crisis mode. People's lives were at stake, and in fact two died. The ripple effects of the emergency would be felt for years. An emergency at this level of seriousness inevitably provokes a crisis-level reaction.

Though emergencies may or may not precipitate a crisis, disasters, by their very nature, do. They represent a massive disruption of life for large numbers of people. They tax response systems to, and often beyond, their limits. They can come as natural disasters—like hurricanes, tornadoes, earthquakes, and tsunamis—or they can result from the failure of human systems—such as electrical power outages, levee breaches, oil rig explosions, or nuclear power plant meltdowns. However they come, they carry significant destructive force. People lose their lives, their homes, their neighborhoods, and their businesses. Entire populations can get wiped off the map or radically altered, as evidenced by the earthquakes in Haiti, Chile, and Japan and the post–Hurricane Katrina developments in New Orleans.

Trauma. "Trauma" comes from a Greek word that means "wound." In medicine it refers to a serious and body-altering injury. In psychology it refers to an emotional injury, usually resulting from an extremely stressful or life-threatening situation. Those caught in the path of the tornado that struck Tuscaloosa, Alabama, on April 24, 2011, suffered trauma of one or both kinds, as did some of those involved in emergency response and disaster relief. Trauma is like that; it can affect the victims, their families, bystanders, and those intensely involved in critical response.

Proximity, however, is not the only factor to consider when looking for those who are traumatized. Some of those closest to the scene of events will come away without feeling traumatized. Others, though somewhat removed, may experience trauma intensely. Personal factors also account for these variations in how people respond.

The effects of psychological trauma can show up immediately or long after the precipitating event and can range from mild to severe. After a traumatic event, affected people, whatever their outward symptoms, must receive immediate support. Posttraumatic stress responds well to timely, personal, skilled intervention.[5] The goals of this intervention are to get people stabilized, facilitate their understanding of what occurred, help them problem solve, and encourage their independent functioning.[6]

Trauma is not a purely personal affair. Groups of people as well as individuals experience it. Congregational consultant Jill Hudson defines trauma as "the large-scale effect of a sudden, unexpected crisis event on a large group of people—namely, the system we call a *congregation.*"[7] As we lead through congregational crisis, we must factor in these personal and corporate dimensions of trauma.

Grief. Trauma response and grief response are related but separate issues. Posttraumatic stress has to do with the disruption of a person's functioning in the aftermath of traumatic events. Grief has to do with the distress one experiences in response to loss.

Crises inevitably bring loss, whatever their nature or scale. We lose loved ones. We lose property. We lose innocence. We lose trust. In crisis something is always lost, and usually those losses are many. When a husband loses a wife, for instance, he has lost a friend, a lover, a confidant, a source of social position, his identity as husband, and any number of other things. When a congregation loses its sanctuary to fire, it has lost worship space, a piece of its heritage, a visible expression of its identity, and a cherished site of personal and congregational memories.

Crises bring loss, and loss brings grief. An essential ingredient of our leadership through a congregational crisis is helping people come to terms with their losses. As with intervention related to trauma, our interventions will be personal and organizational. In congregational crises, we grieve individually and together, and the healing of our corporate grief is essential to our recovery. When we have accepted our losses and reached the point when we can, with sincerity and enthusiasm, embrace a new vision of our future under God, then we know that our crisis has come to an end.

Crisis = Danger + Opportunity?

You may have read or heard someone say that the Chinese word for "crisis" comes by combining the Chinese symbols for "danger" and "opportunity." Victor Mair, professor of Chinese language and literature at the University of Pennsylvania, insists otherwise. Though the first symbol does mean "danger," the second symbol is better translated as "incipient moment" or "crucial point (when something begins or changes)." According to Professor Mair, when crisis is used in Chinese, "the possibility of a highly undesirable outcome (whether in life, disease, finance, or war) is uppermost in the mind of the person who invokes this potent term." He cautions against the pop-culture temptation to misappropriate a Chinese term to create "a feel-good attitude toward adversity."[8]

Let's grant this sobering perspective on pop terminology. At the same time, let's not ignore the underlying truth that a crisis, by putting us at a crossroads, allows for positive as well as negative outcomes. Furthermore, let's not ignore that there *are* opportunities tucked within the unwelcome circumstances that a crisis brings. Biblical faith, in fact, encourages us to see crisis as a prelude to potential good.

Biblical Perspectives on Crisis

Much of the Bible emerges in crisis, whether in the conflicts and crises of the patriarchs in Genesis, the highs and lows of Israel from Exodus to exile, the tragedy and triumph of Jesus as recounted in the gospels, or the persecution and promise of the early church reflected in every book from Acts to Revelation. At each point, biblical faith meets crisis with hope:

- Joseph, with the benefit of hindsight, sees the positive side of his brothers selling him into slavery: "Even though you intended to do harm to me, God intended it for good, in order to preserve a numerous people, as he is doing today" (Genesis 50:20).
- Even in the midst of abysmal failure and misfortune, the people of Israel, exiled in Babylon, received encouragement from God: "For surely I know the plans I have for you, says the LORD, plans for your welfare and not for harm, to give you a future with hope" (Jeremiah 29:11).
- The author of Hebrews, offering guidance in the face of hardship, encourages fellow Christians to

Run with perseverance the race that is set before us, looking to Jesus the pioneer and perfecter of our faith, who for the sake of the joy that was set before him endured the cross, disregarding its shame, and has taken his seat at the right hand of the throne of God. (Hebrews 12:1–2)

Perhaps the apostle Paul captures this spirit best when he responds to the difficulties of the early church by writing, "We know that in all things God works for the good of those who love God, who are called according to his purpose" (Romans 8:28, author's translation).

Crises come; they're part of life. But from faith's perspective, God works with redemptive purpose in the midst of a crisis, so we can confront our crises with confidence about God's intended outcomes.

Kinds of Crisis

Whether personal or organizational, a crisis can be classified as one of three basic types of crisis: *developmental, existential,* and *situational.*[9]

Developmental crises come in the normal course of a person's or organization's life cycle, from birth to old age and death. They have to do with the predictable changes that occur during shifts from one stage to the next. That there's a certain predictability to developmental crises doesn't make them any easier to manage. They can still prove deeply disruptive.

Many factors will impact how quickly and how well a person or organization moves through them. Consider, for example, a man's midlife crisis or a church's turmoil when a younger generation begins to supplant the older generation in shaping the direction of the church.

Existential crises have to do with escalating anxiety over issues of meaning, vision, and values. Individuals may find themselves questioning their core convictions or feeling like they have no worth to the world around them. Organizations may experience a collective loss of vision or find themselves in a corporate struggle over the beliefs and priorities that will guide them. "Who are we?" "Why do we exist?" These questions erupt in an existential crisis. Congregations can find themselves in an existential crisis, for instance, when sharp disagreements arise over whether to focus on the needs of members or guests first. How will our understanding of God's mission affect the things we do? Which of our programs and practices will we preserve and which will we change?

Situational crises occur because of unexpected, extraordinary events that interrupt the normal course of life. By their very nature, these kinds of crises cause a sudden shock to the system, whether personal (as in the cases of death, injury, and divorce) or organizational (as in the cases of the loss of a leader, financial downturn, and sexual misconduct).

This book focuses on leading congregations through situational crises. It provides direction for those who must lead when unwelcome storms, literal or figurative, interrupt the life and work of their congregation.

Readers wanting suggestions for looking more closely at the developmental and existential crises that impact congregations can discover helpful insight in George Bullard's book, *Pursuing the Full Kingdom Potential of Your Congregation.*[10] Bullard looks closely at life-cycle issues that arise for congregations and faith-based organizations. He offers guidance on how to address these issues to experience missional renewal and growth.

Bullard's book also deals with congregations in existential crisis. This topic has become a fertile field of inquiry (though seldom does the term itself–"existential crisis"–come up in the discussion). Much has been made of the seismic culture shifts that are challenging the western church and are forcing local congregations and church-related organizations to rethink their vision, values, and ways of doing things.[11]

Situational Crises Come in Many Shapes and Sizes

Some kinds of situational crisis can strike a church with hammer-like speed and force:

- *Eruptions of violence.* On Sunday, February 14, 2010, a man opens fire during a worship service at New Gethsemane Church in the San Francisco Bay Area, wounding two teenagers.

- *Natural disasters.* Hurricane Charley, one of the strongest hurricanes in recorded history, slams into Punta Gorda, Florida, on Friday the thirteenth, August 2004. Among the many suffering damage is Congregational United Church of Christ.[12]
- *Accidents and medical emergencies.* A bus trip to summer camp takes a tragic turn for twenty-three youth and adult sponsors from First Baptist Church, Shreveport, Louisiana. The bus flips, killing two and leaving others seriously injured.
- *Sudden death.* The thirty-three-year-old pastor of University Baptist Church in Waco, Texas, is electrocuted and dies on October 30, 2005, after he grabs a microphone while in a baptistery full of water.[13]
- *Personnel problems.* The personnel committee of a church in Alexandria, Virginia, fires an associate minister after years of service and offers little by way of explanation, citing confidentiality concerns. Angry church members demand an accounting.
- *Money woes.* A congregation in North Carolina carries out a successful fundraising campaign and begins its construction and remodeling project only to discover that the church treasurer has siphoned off more than $500,000 from the account.
- *Sexual misconduct.* The senior pastor of New Life Church, Colorado Springs, Colorado, is accused of paying a male escort for sex for three years and also of using methamphetamine. He resigns in disgrace.[14]
- *Community trauma.* The American auto industry's difficulties become acute in 2008, causing a severe economic downturn for the already struggling Detroit area. Crosspointe Meadows Church in Novi, Michigan, finds itself wrestling with how to serve its members and its community while dealing with its own budget problems.[15]
- *Legal difficulties.* In 2007, Lake Washington Christian Church in Kirkland, Washington, finds itself at odds with the Transportation Department, which wants its property for freeway expansion.
- *Congregational conflict.* In 2008, a church in Toms River, New Jersey, finds itself embroiled in conflict when five of its members orchestrate an effort to oust the pastor, another staff member, and the existing church board.

In each of these circumstances, a church finds itself off-balance and at risk. Depending on the scope of the crisis and the church's overall resourcefulness, it can even find its very existence in jeopardy.

Congregational Crises: The Ultimate Test

When situational crises occur, the normal patterns of congregational life come under intense pressure. Often, they have to yield to the exigencies of the moment. The congregations that do best under these extraordinary circumstances are the ones that rally around their strengths and guard against their vulnerabilities, all the while pressing into their challenges with confidence in God.

This doesn't happen by accident. When congregations do well in response to crisis, it's a good bet that God has blessed them with effective, caring leaders and the management wherewithal to do what needs to be done.

Reflection Questions

Reflect personally on the following questions. If you are using this book in a study group, share your perspectives with each other.

- What does your faith tell you about how God is at work in crisis?
- What difference does your faith perspective make in the way you respond to and lead through crisis?

3

Leadership, Management, and Crisis Care

Getting Them Right . . . Together

When situational crises strike, congregations need strong leadership. They also need effective management and crisis care. Though these three functions overlap, important characteristics distinguish them. Our effectiveness as congregational leaders depends, in part, on our ability to keep these distinctions clear. Otherwise, we can think we're leading when we're not; we can mistake activity for progress; and we can shortchange the potential for personal and congregational development that lies waiting in the disruptive circumstances with which we contend.

Doing the Right Things; Doing Things Right

Let's begin by dealing with the distinctions between leadership and management. The father of modern management, Peter Drucker, once observed that leadership is "doing the right things," whereas management is "doing things right."[1] This pithy way of framing the comparison may seem a bit simplistic, but it actually gets at an essential distinction between these key roles in crisis response.

Leadership Is Doing the Right Things

Leaders are custodians of mission, vision, and values. They must remain clear about the big picture that drives the congregation. They bear special responsibility to keep the organization on mission, clarify priorities, and make sure the church is stewarding its God-given vision and values, come what may.

Under normal circumstances this can prove difficult. As leadership expert Stephen Covey discusses, the urgent has a way of trumping the important, especially when what's important isn't urgent.[2]

I have found this to be true throughout my years of ministry. The weekly calendar fills quickly with deadlines, meetings, and appointments. We spend our days coordinating worship plans with other worship leaders; preparing to preach and teach; attending and leading congregational gatherings (worship and otherwise); writing for congregational publications; and facilitating staff meetings, committee meetings, and personal appointments. Beyond these duties, outreach and pastoral care call for attention, as do mail, e-mail, and other forms of social networking.

Whether the congregation is large or small, urban or rural, congregational life presents ample opportunity for the minutiae of everyday ministry to crowd out strategic reflection. What happens over time, if we're not careful, is that a disconnect develops between the things we're doing and the outcomes we desire. We can actually get better and better at driving in circles.

Effective leaders make sure this doesn't happen. They cultivate their capacity for reflection in the midst of action. Ronald Heifitz and Marty Linsky call this "getting off the dance floor and going to the balcony."[3] Sometimes this means taking a time out and physically removing oneself to a quiet place of contemplation. Sometimes it means remaining where the action is while stepping back in one's mind to gain a clearer view of reality and a fresh perspective on the bigger picture.

In crisis stepping back becomes more important than ever, even as doing so becomes more difficult. The urgencies of the hour can become all-consuming. It takes strong leadership to remain strategically focused when chaos breaks loose. Effective combat officers are particularly adept at this. They remain mission focused and tactically nimble under the intense pressures of the battlefield, leading those under their command to fulfill their objectives while responding adaptively to continuously changing circumstances.[4]

Congregational leaders cultivate the same capacity. They keep their heads and maintain their congregations' focus when crises threaten to distract them. They keep their congregations on track when traumas threaten to derail them.

Leadership is about ensuring that the congregation is doing the right things.

Management Is Doing Things Right

Management plays a complementary role to leadership. Assuming leaders maintain clarity about *what* needs to happen, managers focus on *how* to make it happen and happen right. They orchestrate the processes that get things done in a timely and efficient way. Managers bear responsibility for detailing plans and seeing them through to completion. It has been said that "the devil is in the details." When it comes to a congregation's ability to weather its crises, it might better be said that "*God* is in the details and acts through the steady hands of those who *do things right.*"

In the aftermath of the bus accident involving First Baptist Shreveport's adult sponsors and youth, Susie Holton played this managerial role in exemplary ways. A volunteer leader with proven organizational skills, Susie agreed on the day of the accident to serve as point person for the caregiving side of our crisis response. At 8:30 the next morning, she met with me and First Baptist's minister of faith formation and administration, Gene Hendrix, to clarify her assignment. She wasted no time fleshing out the details of the plan and putting it into motion. For the next four weeks, she worked tirelessly, marshaling resources and mobilizing members as we tended to the needs of accident victims and their families.

People versus Process

Gene Klann accents a different distinction between crisis leadership and crisis management. Drawing on a distinguished twenty-five-year career in the military and his work as a member of the training faculty of the Center for Creative Leadership, Gene accents the *relational focus* of leadership in contrast with the *task focus* of management. Whereas management concerns itself with operational issues during crisis, leadership concerns itself with human responses to crisis, including the leader's own response.[5] To somewhat oversimplify the point: whereas crisis management is about *process*, crisis leadership is about *people.*

Managers take responsibility for the tasks that need to get done to forestall, mitigate, or resolve crisis. They focus on the tactical side of the equation.

Leaders, by comparison, take responsibility for shaping the way people react and respond to crisis. They focus on the personal and interpersonal side of the equation.

A crisis generates high levels of anxiety, insecurity, and confusion among those who are directly and indirectly touched by the crisis. Leaders use clarity of purpose in combination with interpersonal skills to keep people informed, maintain people's focus on vision and values, and care for them as the crisis moves toward resolution.

Leaders move their organizations through crisis by influencing those whose responses spell the difference between disaster and hope. Crisis leadership is about the ways we use our influence to steer a community of people through difficulty.

Rudy Giuliani, former mayor of New York City, has received almost universal praise for the effectiveness with which he displayed these leadership qualities on and after the terrorist attacks of September 11, 2001. He showed up, making his way immediately to the scene of the disaster to assess the situation, orchestrate response, and demonstrate his confidence in the resilience of New Yorkers. He kept his composure, displaying an empathetic strength that reassured people and helped them think clearly and react appropriately during the crisis. He put his communication gifts to good use, calming people and pointing the way toward an orderly response. He showed resilience. His native optimism, reinforced by years of public leadership, enabled him to face the cataclysmic disaster with irrepressible confidence. He deeply believed that the people of New York, and Americans in general, would rise to the challenge. His resilience enhanced the resilience of New Yorkers and anxious people around the world.[6]

Management is about process; leadership is about people.

Leaders Manage; Managers Lead

Though managing and leading are two distinct functions, they are not mutually exclusive. In reality, leaders manage and managers lead. I mention this because, whether your role makes you primarily one or the other, you will inevitably do both in the course of dealing with an organizational crisis.

If you have primary responsibilities to manage, you will still have to deal with the all-too-human responses to crisis that impact your work, and you will have to exercise leadership as you marshal human resources to implement your tactical response. If you have primary responsibilities to lead, you will still have to deal with tactical issues and monitor progress as things unfold.

It's important to recognize the overlapping nature of leading and managing because you will be wearing both hats throughout the process. You simply need to remain clear about which is which so that, on the one hand, you don't get stuck in the thicket of details and lose sight of where you're headed in the long run, and so that, on the other hand, you don't fail to get where you're going because good intentions didn't translate into effective actions.

Leadership and Crisis Care

Having talked about leadership and management and the complementary roles they play, let's now add crisis care to the mix and remind ourselves that a leadership orientation alters the way we understand and fulfill the caring agenda.

Need we even say it?–Caring is a good thing. Actually, it's an indispensible thing. Leaders who lack emotional intelligence make matters worse. They aggravate human suffering. They look past people when shaping and executing plans. They allow institutional interests to trump basic kindness. Unwittingly, they undermine the very ends they seek.

Crisis response calls for compassion. In crisis, the compassionate heart expresses itself in words and deeds that comfort, guide, and encourage. Caring helps people heal. It promotes their resilience. It renews a spirit of hope. Caring by itself, however, isn't enough. Caring in the absence of leadership turns mercy and help toward the alleviation of suffering, but such caring lacks the imagination to see potential in crisis for

- spiritual formation and transformation,
- congregational development,
- missional innovation.

This type of caring also lacks the discipline and persistence to pursue these possibilities in the face of distractions and complications. Leadership is the ingredient in our caring that keeps these things on the agenda. Without it the transformational potential of crisis goes to waste.

Those of us who serve as shepherd-leaders in crisis can benefit from regular self-assessment related to the three areas of potential just mentioned. We can ask ourselves,

- Is all my attention focused on *alleviating suffering,* or do I help people discover the *transformational potential* in their suffering?
- Do I think of pastoral care solely as a *personal service* to individuals and families, or do I see its *corporate potential* and rally the caring resources of the congregation to promote "building up the body of Christ" (Ephesians 4:11–16)?
- Does my care aim at *returning things to normal,* or does it aim at discovering and *embracing the new normal* toward which God is pulling the congregation?

Over the course of this book, we will get to know leaders whose congregations were severely tested and who met the tests in personally and congregationally advantageous ways. We'll meet leaders like Bill Klossner, whose congregation weathered a destructive hurricane, only to become more intentional than ever about its role in the community; Al Meredith, whose congregation suffered horrendous violence and remained missionally focused while tending to the long-term needs of the bereaved and traumatized; and Danny Langley, whose Detroit-area congregation responded to economic crisis in caring and innovative ways.[7] These and other leaders whose stories appear in these pages have faced a variety of crises, but they share in common the blend of compassion and missional purpose that makes effective congregational leadership possible.

Overview of the Rest of the Book

This book holds leading, managing, and caring in fruitful relationship throughout. At the same time, it leans on the leadership side of the equation. It looks at management and caring through a leader's lens.

How do congregational leaders react when crisis first strikes? How do they deal with the chaos that inevitably ensues? How do they prioritize their work after that first response? What leadership actions make the most difference in the long run? How do leaders leverage crises to strengthen and transform their congregations?

I am grateful to the many congregational leaders who contributed their stories and their wisdom to what follows. The insights in this book represent their hard-earned education in the eye of congregational storms.

Chapter 4 will take an honest look at the kinds of things that occur in congregations when a crisis erupts. It will present guidance for getting a handle on the chaos that initially occurs.

Chapter 5 picks up where the previous chapter ends, focusing on the challenges of crisis leadership during the days, weeks, or even months that follow its initial onset. The material includes frank discussion about the strategic, pastoral, and logistical issues that come into play during congregational recovery.

By its very nature, crisis disrupts the normal life of the church and becomes an all-consuming focus of attention. Furthermore, it creates short-term and long-term ripple effects that must be managed. Chapter 6 discusses what congregations have learned about putting the church back on track in the aftermath of a crisis. It talks about finding a "new normal."

Healthy congregations understand the kingdom potential that lurks beneath the surface of a crisis. Chapter 7 relays how crisis leaders have prompted their congregations to reflect on and experience positive transformation as an outcome of trauma.

Though I could have put the conversation about prevention and preparation first, I decided to save this part of the conversation until chapter 8. For one thing, I wanted this book to be a source of encouragement and help to those of you who have picked this book up because you find yourself in the middle of a crisis *right now.* You don't need someone to tell you what you could have done to prevent or better prepare for what you're facing. You need someone to help you navigate your current situation. My second reason for postponing this chapter until this point is that it builds on chapter 7 with its focus on learning from crisis. For many of the leaders I interviewed, going through a crisis provided the impetus their congregation needed to do risk assessments, to plan so as to prevent preventable crises in the future, and to prepare for crises that might still occur.

Healthy churches are uniquely suited to tend to the spiritual stress that crises provoke and to engage in faith-affirming practices. Chapter 9 elaborates on this fact and offers ideas from crisis leaders for tapping into the power of worship, scripture, prayer, and other corporate expressions of faith.

Leading through crisis without burning out is the focus of chapter 10. Congregational crisis places special pressures on those who lead. This chapter shares what leaders have learned—from getting it right and getting it wrong—about a leader's self-care through crisis.

What's a leader to do when crisis comes crashing in on congregational life? Let's take a closer look.

Reflection Questions

Reflect personally on the following questions. If you are using this book with a study group, share your perspectives with each other.

- Based on the explanations in this chapter, in what ways are you currently a leader? A manager? A caregiver?
- Think of someone you consider an outstanding leader under pressure. Which of their leadership characteristics stand out most to you?
- Reflect on the crisis-care-related questions earlier in this chapter. What outcomes do you hope will result from the way your congregation moves through crisis?

Part II

Crisis Leadership from Onset to Resolution

Congregations in Focus

Wedgwood Baptist Church, Fort Worth, Texas

More than a decade after its crisis, Wedgwood Baptist Church in Fort Worth, Texas, still devotes a page of its Web site to the September 15, 1999, shooting that put it on the media map. That evening, just before 7 p.m., a mentally deranged gunman entered the sanctuary during an area-wide youth rally. He fired more than one hundred rounds from two handguns and exploded a homemade pipe bomb. Seven youth and young adults were killed, and seven others were wounded before the gunman took his own life.

Why the Web site feature more than a decade later? The answer is simple: Wedgwood has transformed its tragedy into a testimony of faith and a service of love. Knowing that the church's notoriety as a result of that night still draws people from around the world to its Web site, Wedgwood has created a link where people can learn more (including access to the complete text of Dan Crawford's now out-of-print book on the crisis, *Night of Tragedy; Dawning of Light*) and hear a message of hope from the pastor, Dr. Al Meredith. His message—"Where Was God?"—is a recording from Sunday, September 19, 1999, four days following the shooting. The Web site includes the following statement:

> Through this tragedy we have gained a new understanding of what is meant when we say, "God is sovereign." He was there during the shootings. He comforts us today as we grieve and as we continue to recover. Through trials He brings understanding; He strengthens our faith when there can be no understanding.
>
> And through it all; in every tragedy, there is Hope, and His name is "Jesus Christ."[1]

At the time of the shooting Meredith was home, having just returned from his mother's funeral. In an ironic kind of way, the numbness of his own grief served him well in the hours and days after the phone call informing him of the disaster. It cushioned him against the trauma and allowed him to focus on the immediate demands of pastoral leadership. *Just do the next thing,* his mind told him. *Go to the police and ask, how can I help? Gather 150 kids to a room; get their statements. Go to the morgue with the families of lost loved ones. Speak to a press conference.* Says Meredith, "I watch a recording of the press conference now, and I can't believe what I said. I was numb."

Of foundational importance for the way Meredith led Wedgwood to respond to the trauma was what he calls catastrophology—a theology of catastrophe. He believes all pastors need to help their people deal with the problem of evil.

> Crisis is spiritual warfare, first and foremost. The issue isn't gun control or the mentally deranged or security processes. As long as the devil's in the world, we're told to expect trials, tribulation, crises. So why bother asking, "Why us?" The better question is, "Why *not* us?"

Not surprisingly, he also points to Jesus' reassuring words in the gospel of John: "In the world you face persecution. But take courage; I have conquered the world!" (John 16:33).

The decision was made on the night of the shooting to worship in the sanctuary on Sunday, only four days later. It was a way of saying, "We will not give an inch to the darkness." Crime scene tape had to be discarded. Bloodied carpet and some of the pews had to be removed. Debris had to be picked up and swept away. Bullet holes had to be patched. Walls had to be repainted. After this, members of the church prayed their way through the whole building. Those who participated in worship that Sunday morning describe it as one of the most electric, spiritually rich worship experiences they can ever remember.

In the weeks following that memorable Sunday, Meredith preached a six-week series on congregational purpose to keep people focused. Against every impulse to give into fear or anger, the people of Wedgwood were encouraged to remember who they were—the people of God—and what they were to do—know Christ and make him known. In the midst of their crisis they called on their God-given mission as a way to stay focused and faithful. They also called on it as they sought to respond with Christlike grace and forgiveness.

Money came in from people everywhere—more than $250,000—and that, combined with another $100,000 from the Tarrant Baptist Association, became the primary source of funding for member counseling, given the number of people traumatized by the event and the depth of their trauma. The church insisted that all staff and their spouses go to counselors.

They were told to expect it to take five years for posttraumatic stress to peak. Says Meredith, even now, "We haven't gotten over it, but we have gotten through it." He still, for instance, has to calm panicky parents from time to time. He credits the larger body of Christ for its role in healing: "There was a period of time during which we were the most prayed for church in the world!"

Little changed in the way Wedgwood carried out its ministries after the shooting. "We were doing what we needed to do," says Meredith. Congregational leaders had been warned that after trauma like this one, many churches "blow up," but Wedgwood actually experienced a 50 percent growth over the next five years.

How about its handling of security matters? Has this event changed the way Wedgwood manages risk? In keeping with its commitment to keep things in perspective, Wedgwood has taken what it considers reasonable precautions, without caving into a fortress mentality. A subcommittee of their administrative committee focuses on risk-related concerns. For example, they make sure that the church has adequate insurance and up-to-date policies related to the screening of those who work with children and youth. They are currently in conversations about security cameras at designated locations in and around their buildings.

Wedgwood is committed to reasonable security measures, but they know that there's not enough money to screen everyone who comes onto the campus. In fact, they know that if a church only lets "safe people" in, they will miss opportunities that come with being God's instruments of light and love.

Recently, a skinhead showed up at church. His appearance and behavior was somewhat unnerving, and he didn't stay very long once the worship service began. He returned the next Sunday, however, and by his third visit he managed to stay through the sermon. He never would have made it into some churches' buildings, given their security practices. Among the people of Wedgwood he still has a chance to experience God.[2]

4

When Crisis Strikes

Dealing with Chaos

When the mentally deranged gunman entered the sanctuary doors of Wedgwood Baptist Church that Wednesday night in 1999, all hell broke loose. Those in attendance for the area-wide youth rally initially thought they were witnessing a dramatic enactment. It soon became clear that these were deadly serious circumstances. Panic and chaos reigned as the shooting continued. Some hid under the pews while others ran for their lives. Bullets struck fourteen youth and young adults. Seven of those wounded would die. Even after the gunman ended his deadly shooting spree by taking his own life, trauma and confusion remained. The sheer magnitude of the disaster created a mountainous challenge.

Despite differences from crisis to crisis, all crises share certain characteristics. The first characteristic they share is that to one degree or another, every crisis catches the congregation off guard and throws it into a state of confusion.

The first consequence of crisis is chaos.

Leadership in the Midst of Chaos

Wedgwood's pastor, Dr. Al Meredith, faced particularly difficult circumstances that night. Nonetheless, those circumstances and his response to them provide lessons for other congregations and leaders going through crisis.

The key to effective leadership at the outset of a crisis is the ability to step into the chaos and get the situation under control. Crisis containment is the first priority and calls for

1. a cool head,
2. a warm heart,
3. a built-in bias for action.

Your ability to balance these three qualities will enable you to confront the situation head-on and do what the moment calls for you to do.

A Cool Head

In his poem "If," Rudyard Kipling extolled the ability to "keep your head when all about you are losing theirs."[1] Not only do others need to see your calm, but calmness of spirit allows you to assess the situation more effectively and think through your response. You want to avoid wasting unnecessary time and energy by overreacting or giving into feeling over-whelmed. Accept the fact that chaos is inevitable, that it's natural to feel confused, and that you're dealing with an ill-defined, moving target.

Christian leaders have a distinct advantage here. By faith we know that though we aren't in control, God is. Furthermore, we draw on the assurance that God is with us in the midst of these unsettled, unsettling circumstances. Psalm 46 reminds us that "God is our refuge and strength, a very present help in trouble" (Psalm 46:1, KJV).

Jesus buoys our spirits by telling us, "In the world you face persecution. But take courage; I have conquered the world!" (John 16:33). The apostle Paul encourages us by informing us, "No testing has overtaken you that is not common to everyone. God is faithful, and he will not let you be tested beyond your strength, but with the testing he will also provide a way out so that you may be able to endure it" (1 Corinthians 10:13). Our ability to collect ourselves becomes a priceless gift in a time of high stress.

Get past shock and denial. A crisis, by its very nature, creates a shock to the body's system. One's mind sometimes has difficulty absorbing the truth of what is actually happening; one's emotions take time to catch up.

Pastor Meredith remembers how numb he felt when the call came telling him of the gunman's attack at his church. The combination of his grief from his mom's recent death and the stunning nature of the circumstances anesthetized him. He counted it as one of God's small blessings in the midst of the trauma that his numbness allowed him to move into the chaos and simply do what needed doing.

Though the circumstances of First Baptist Shreveport's bus accident were very different from the ones Meredith faced, I remember a similar sense of numbness when Maria Webb came running to me with news of what had happened. I also remember an element of internal resistance to the news, a kind of "this can't be happening!" response. Something in me wanted to minimize the potential implications of what I was hearing. Something in me wanted this to be nothing more than a momentary little inconvenience, so that everything about life and the church could keep rocking along unfazed. In other words, I experienced denial.

Another set of instincts kicked in almost immediately, driven by the realization that because our church's two worship services were about to begin, several important decisions had to be made without delay:

- Who would lead worship in the sanctuary? The daughter of the scheduled preacher, Associate Pastor John Henson, had been seriously injured in the accident, and he was leaving immediately to be with her.
- How would the news be handled with the congregation?
- What shape would each worship service take?
- Would I stick with my plans for worship leadership or alter them?

Even though I felt numb and my mind struggled to absorb what I was hearing, another side of me knew that I didn't have the luxury of ignoring the dramatic nature of the moment.

However much we may want to pretend that a crisis isn't happening, however much we may want to put all the scattered pieces back in the box and get back to normal, we have to accept that this isn't possible. It's not going to happen! The sooner we accept this fact the better. We have to gear up and get our head in the game.

Face the facts. Our ability to remain calm puts us in a position to push past shock and denial and get the information we need for effective response. We have to know what we're dealing with if we're going to respond appropriately.

Facing the facts means, first and foremost, getting accurate information. At the outset of a crisis, the details are often sketchy, confusion reigns, and circumstances may continue to change rapidly. This is the congregational equivalent of what military leaders call the fog of war. The ability to get accurate, timely information becomes crucial to effective crisis response.

When word came of our bus accident, we knew almost nothing other than that an accident had occurred. Where had it happened? What caused it? How serious was it? What had become of each of those on the bus? What was their current condition? Where was the bus? What was its present condition? Whom could we contact to get information? On and on the questions came. More than anything else at that point, we needed answers to these questions. We needed answers so we could begin organizing our response, informing our people, and praying with clarity of purpose.

Our first concern was for those who had been on the bus. To our good fortune, the pastor of First Baptist Church (FBC), Meridian, Mississippi, learned of the accident only minutes after it occurred and understood how important this information was. He took it upon himself to locate all twenty three of those who had been on the bus and get an update on their condition. He also provided us with other helpful information that only an on-the-ground person could provide. He and his staff continued to update us as the first day of the crisis unfolded.

Either formally or informally, this early process of facing the facts will include an assessment of the level of the crisis. Crisis management expert Laurence Barton suggests three potential levels for the severity of an incident:

1. *Minor incident.* An occurrence of this nature doesn't qualify as a congregation-wide crisis, though it may create real concern. When an elderly member loses her balance and falls while on the church premises and breaks her wrist, those in a position to do so take immediate action to comfort her and get her into the hands of medical professionals. Follow-up involves pastoral care and attentiveness about insurance needs—hers and the church's. Under normal circumstances, this event remains isolated. It doesn't affect the overall functioning of the church.

2. *Emergency.* Any incident that seriously disrupts the overall life of the church qualifies as an emergency. The FBC Shreveport bus accident fits this description. It became a matter of obsessive concern for an extended period of time, despite the things we did to continue the normal ministries of the church.

3. *Disaster.* A disaster ratchets things up yet another level. It seriously impairs or threatens the church's ability to continue functioning at all. Churches in southern Louisiana experienced crisis at this level in the aftermath of Hurricane Katrina. With their buildings seriously damaged, their members scattered to locations across the country, and communication systems disrupted, many churches didn't know for sure if their congregations would survive. Some, in fact, didn't.[2]

Accept responsibility. To deal constructively with the facts that come in, you must own responsibility. You have no time for passing off blame or acting powerless. The basic posture has to be, "We will face the facts, accept our share of responsibility for what occurred, *and* take full responsibility for how we respond."

Sometimes this means taking responsibility for things that have happened because of neglect or failure. The personnel committee of Holmeswood Baptist Church, the church I pastored in Kansas City, Missouri, attempted to fast-track a decision to shift from a part-time to a full-time minister of music. The committee—and I as an ex officio member of the committee—failed to have a private conversation with the part-time minister of music before the plan went public. Jack had been in the position for more than a decade, but wouldn't be a candidate for the position because he already had a full-time job as a high school music teacher. He, his family, and loyal friends—especially choir members—reacted strongly and negatively to the news.

Those involved in the decision met quickly and surveyed the situation. We took public responsibility for failing to communicate effectively with the minister of music before word got out to the church, and we slowed the decision-making process down so we could enter more effectively into dialogue with those most impacted by the recommendation. This took some pressure off the process. The recommendation ultimately carried the day. I also took private steps to deal with the relational damage that had been done between me and the minister of music.

When our neglect or failure causes a crisis, we need to accept responsibility immediately and act ethically when dealing with the consequences of our mistake.

On the other hand, the fault for many situational crises doesn't fall at our feet. We may be victims, as was the case when Hurricane Charley wreaked havoc on the community of Punta Gorda, Florida, and damaged churches like Congregational United Church of Christ (CUCC). In situations like this, we have no apologies to make, nor do we have an excuse to remain stuck in the role of victim. The sooner we accept responsibility for what happens *next*, the better. Such acceptance speeds our ability to get on top of the situation and improve the circumstances. Pastor Bill Klossner led CUCC in swift, decisive action.

Consider, by way of corporate example, the response of Johnson & Johnson after the 1982 Tylenol scare. In October 1982, seven people in the Chicago area were reported dead from taking cyanide-laced Extra-Strength Tylenol capsules. Despite clear evidence that the deadly tampering had occurred after the product was placed on store shelves, Johnson & Johnson, as the makers of Tylenol, decided to get in front of the situation immediately. They issued a total product recall and produced tamper-proof packaging before putting the product back into circulation. This decision cost them $100 million. They placed public safety ahead of their pride and their short-term economic interests.

A Warm Heart

The counterpart to a cool head is a warm heart. As already established, crisis leadership is an intensely relational process. It calls on us to serve those most directly impacted by the crisis, deal with people's anxiety, address their questions and concerns, and provide encouragement and hope.

Show caring concern. In a time of crisis, most pastoral leaders put their pastoral-care-in-crisis skills, training, and experience into play instinctively.[3] They think relationally and empathetically. They understand the power and the vulnerabilities of community. They spend prime energy providing comfort and encouragement.

On Sunday, November 4, 2007, when the 103-year-old sanctuary of Sandy Run Baptist Church in Hampton, South Carolina, went up in flames, Pastor Paul Reid was on-site to embrace tearful members upon their arrival. Gathering people at the softball-field bleachers just beyond the church parking lot, Reid milled among them to hear their stories and share their pain.

His pastoral instincts and his warm heart provided much-needed solace to traumatized people (Sandy Run's experience with crisis and renewal is captured in chapter 9's "Congregations in Focus").

Depending on the size of the church and the nature of the crisis, this caring work may be done solo or through a caring team. The pastor's ability to mobilize a caring team (and in many cases, to bless those who have already stepped in to care) can strengthen a congregation's compassionate response.

Put people first. The idea of putting people first would seem to go without saying, given the focus of our interests as congregational leaders. Honesty forces us to acknowledge, however, that our concern for the well-being of people can come into tension with our concerns for self and the institutional interests of the church. These other concerns can get in the way of making people our top priority.

As an extreme example, consider the sexual abuse scandal that has rocked the Roman Catholic Church. A 2004 study commissioned by the U.S. Conference of Bishops surfaced 10,667 allegations against 4,392 priests engaging in sexual abuse of a minor between 1950 and 2002. The bishops investigated 6,696 of the cases further, and 80 percent of the allegations were substantiated.[4] Making matters worse, in many of these cases, members of the Catholic hierarchy failed to report abuse allegations to civil authorities and even reassigned offenders to other locations where they had ongoing contact with minors and further opportunities for sexual abuse.[5]

Congregational leaders of any tradition can fall prey to the temptation to put their self-interests and the self-interests of the institution ahead of the needs of the people who look to them in trust. They can allow concerns over such things as cost, inconvenience, embarrassment, and fear of litigation to color the way they handle crises. Putting people first, then, is a matter not only of compassion but of character.

The idea of putting people first isn't an idea exclusive to congregational ministry. It has a prominent place in business-related books on crisis leadership too. The Harvard Business Essentials book *Crisis Management* states,

> Make people your first concern. In the end, material things can be replaced—and most are already insured against loss . . . [W]ithin the bounds of good sense, don't worry about the budget or the other workplace procedures that govern how things are done under normal conditions. Instead, do what it takes to keep people safe.[6]

A Built-in Bias for Action

Those involved in emergency medicine refer to "the golden hour," a time period immediately after a traumatic injury during which there is the highest likelihood that prompt medical treatment will prevent death. The term doesn't necessarily refer to a literal sixty-minute time frame. Depending on the nature of the injury, the golden hour may actually last anywhere from a few minutes to several hours. Nevertheless, the term accents the fact that with a serious injury, prompt medical intervention has a significant impact on health outcomes.[7]

Act quickly and decisively. The idea of the golden hour translates well at the onset of congregational crises. When crises erupt, leaders have important decisions to make and must make some of them as soon as possible. Al Meredith didn't have the luxury of time when the phone call came alerting him to violence at the church. He had to absorb the shocking news, get as much information as he could as quickly as he could, and move into action. When he arrived at the church, he had to do continuous assessment while dealing with the needs of the traumatized, cooperating with emergency responders, and addressing the media. He also had to begin thinking ahead about the congregation's immediate future. It was Wednesday night; the sanctuary was in bloody shambles and Sunday morning was only four days away.

Indicative of Meredith's decisiveness was his response that very night to the question of where the congregation would gather for worship on Sunday. He considered it a matter of first importance that the congregation reclaim its worship space for God and demonstrate that it would not be cowed by evil. He understood the implications of this for the congregation's emotional healing as well. While working collaboratively with staff and other congregational leaders, Meredith brought timely leadership to the situation and played an essential role in restoring order.

To infer from this that the congregation had only one correct way to handle the Sunday worship question would be a mistake. In fact, after Pastor Kyle Lake's tragic death by electrocution in the baptistery in October 2005, the leadership of University Baptist Church (UBC) in Waco, Texas, decided to postpone its return to its sanctuary for months, even after it had been cleared for use by safety inspectors. They decided to continue meeting at alternate locations and remodel the sanctuary first. The leaders of Wedgwood and UBC each faced unique circumstances, and they had their own reasons for the decisions they made. In both cases, they took responsibility as decision leaders in the midst of extraordinary circumstances that demanded a judgment call.

Based on twenty-five years of military command, crisis expert Gene Klann explains,

> During a crisis, even a wrong decision that promotes action is better than doing nothing. Influential decision making means gathering information and getting input as soon as possible, knowing that all the information needed to make the decision isn't available, accepting that there are risks involved, getting recommendations from others, listening to gut feelings, and making the decision because it needs to be made.[8]

Leaders stand a better chance of doing this well if they can manage their emotions when stress is at its peak. They must stay calm, face the facts, and accept responsibility as improvisational decision makers.

Be present. As former U.S. president George W. Bush knows from personal leadership experience, the need for decisiveness in the throes of crisis must be coupled with presence. He was universally praised for showing up at "ground zero" in New York City soon after the devastating terrorist attacks of September 9, 2001, and roundly criticized for failing to put his feet on the ground in southern Louisiana for almost a week following Hurricane Katrina in August 2005.

When crisis strikes, the built-in bias for action includes moving to the center of the action, wherever that happens to be. People need to see that their leaders are present and undaunted by the unfortunate developments. Circumstances demand a leader's command presence.

This was a consistent theme in the interviews I conducted with crisis leaders. These leaders showed up and stayed present. Pastor Paul Reid of Sandy Run Baptist Church even set up his SUV in front of the burned-out church and continued to keep office hours there for months!

The leader operates in a setting where people are in turmoil, emotionally distraught, and floundering for answers and solid footing. People are reassured and encouraged to act similarly when the leader steps in confidently, is heard as a soothing voice, and is seen as a steady hand. Edwin Friedman coined the term "nonanxious presence" to describe this capability.[9]

Rally response. A leader's steadying presence has intrinsic power. At the onset of a crisis, it sets up something more. As soon as feasible, leaders must empower people and mobilize response. They do this for the sake of the situation itself and everyone involved in the crisis, including themselves.

The situation itself calls for broad-based involvement. A crisis is a congregation-wide problem, and a congregation-wide problem demands a congregation-wide response. In seafaring terms, it calls for all hands on deck. In November 2006, when founding pastor Ted Haggard stepped down in disgrace from New Life Church in Colorado Springs, Colorado, music ministry pastor Ross Parsley, functioning in the role of interim pastor, called for members to join him at the church for early morning prayer five days a week. This daily time of prayer continued through the holidays. Parsley knew that the church's future depended on its responsiveness to the leadership of God's Spirit.

Rallying response is essential for the church itself. *Furthermore, it meets a need in people.* Crises throw us off balance and make us feel like we've lost control. They can immobilize us with confusion, uncertainty, and fear. The sooner we have something to do that empowers us again, the sooner we will regain our footing. Concrete action is good for morale.

Concrete action also channels the compassion of members. In every crisis through which I've led, one of the first questions members ask is,

"What can we do?" Effective leadership at the outset of a crisis includes giving people specific instructions so they know what to do next. In fact, in the absence of clear, concrete guidance, people will find things to do, whether those things are truly helpful or not.

In the aftermath of Hurricane Katrina, some sixty thousand southern Louisianans landed on the doorstep of Shreveport-Bossier City. We, the members of FBC Shreveport, joined volunteers from across the metropolitan area to respond to their needs. Before we could even fully organize our response, well-meaning people from across the country began sending truckloads of food, clothing, and other supplies, some of it not even needed. Among the challenges with which we had to cope was deciding where to store and how to dispense these contributions. Months later, when the crisis had abated, disaster relief coordinators had to figure out what to do with warehouses full of unused clothing and household furnishings.

The pent-up need to do something must be channeled in ways that actually contribute to rather than complicate the recovery process. As time goes by, the opportunities for constructive action will become clearer and increase in number. In the immediate aftermath of a crisis-precipitating event, people can still do helpful things—pray, give, provide personal care to those most directly affected by the crisis, and so on. We as leaders need to make these options for action clear.

If handled well, the rallying of response has an additional benefit, beyond that of meeting the needs of the church and the people. *It also meets the need of the one rallying response.* In his book *7 Lessons for Leading in Crisis,* Harvard management professor and former Medtronic CEO Bill George devotes a chapter to this insight. His second lesson of crisis leadership is "Don't be Atlas; get the world off your shoulders." He counsels,

> You cannot get through this alone, so don't try to carry the whole world on your shoulders. Reach out to others inside your organization and in your personal life to share the burden and help you come out a winner. This is a great opportunity to strengthen chemistry within your team, because the strongest bonds are built in crisis.[10]

George's comment has implications not only for collaborative leadership but also for a leader's self-care during the challenging period of a crisis. I will have more to say about this in chapter 10.

A crisis management team. For now, let's focus on the matter of the leader's vested interest in collaborative leadership. During my conversations with crisis leaders, I heard wide variations in the ways they handled this important issue. Those who withstood the pressures best either had an established crisis management team or put one together quickly, drawing on the expertise of those who could add their complementary strengths to the challenge.

When worship ended on the morning of FBC Shreveport's bus accident, I moved immediately to our church office to turn my attention to information gathering and response. When I arrived in the office area, several staff members and other concerned members stood present and ready to help. Among these were the deacon chair (an attorney), two newspaper people, a television reporter, a member who had experience operating the church's phone system, and others with time to make calls to the families of those involved in the accident. These volunteers, in addition to the pastoral staff, played crucial roles in dealing with the crisis. Within hours, I was able to put together the core team of leaders who would provide tactical guidance for the full length of our crisis response.

If you don't already have a collaborative team for handling crisis, you will want to form one as soon as you can. The team with whom you work may be an elected body in the church, such as the board of elders, the body of deacons, trustees, the church council, or a standing committee with special interest in the particular crisis. It may be a special task force established as part of a planning process for crisis prevention and preparation. The team might be pulled together after a crisis has erupted. The key is to start with what you've got in terms of readily available leadership and activate the group immediately.

If, for any reason, you find yourself flying solo as a leader, consider it a matter of the utmost importance to secure a support person or two as soon as you can, even if you have to look outside the congregation to identify one. Ecclesiastes reminds, "Two are better than one, because they have a good return for their toil . . . A threefold cord is not quickly broken" (Ecclesiastes 4:9, 12). One person can't think of everything, and the burden of crisis leadership is too heavy for going it alone.

Collaboration in and beyond the congregation. If you're a leader in a smaller church, you will not have the same support options as do the leaders of larger churches. You will still have options, and you need to call on them. Depending on the nature of the crisis, churches of all sizes also need to think beyond the church membership when calling for support. Ben Dudley, community pastor of UBC of Waco, wasted no time calling for inside and outside support in the aftermath of Kyle's death. Word of the tragedy reached the news media quickly. When Dudley began receiving phone calls from reporters, he turned to UBCer and Baylor University assistant professor of communication studies, Dr. Blair Browning, for guidance. Browning continued to play a vital role in UBC's handling of internal and external communications. Ben also got support from a sister congregation, FBC of Waco, to host a remembrance of Kyle for UBCers and others from the community that first night.

Getting through the Night

"Getting through the night" is a term used frequently in crisis counseling. It has applications for the whole process of getting a congregation through the initial shock of crisis. It recognizes that in the heat of crisis, people tend to feel overwhelmed. Under these circumstances, we remind ourselves to take one day at a time, to bite off one piece at a time. This isn't the time to make long-term decisions or to rework congregational mission, vision, or values. This is the time to lean on existing mission, vision, and values and focus on the urgent, practical needs of the moment.

Crisis is a time for something like triage—a process that involves assessing the nature and extent of the crisis and prioritizing initial response. Even here, leaders operate bifocally. With one eye we focus on the situation at hand and do whatever it takes to stabilize the patient, in this case our church. With the other eye we focus on the long-term interests of the church. We never want to lose sight of why we exist, what values matter most to us, and where God has pointed us.

This means that we can't be overly simplistic about "getting through the night," lest we jury-rig short-term solutions that take the church off mission or that complicate things for us unnecessarily in the long run. Again, I think of Al Meredith's clarity of conviction and how it steeled the church to move right back into its patterns of worship and ministry. They took immediate steps to deal with the horrific condition of the sanctuary after the massacre, and they managed to worship there four days after the tragedy. They put plans into play immediately to deal with the psychological needs of victims, families, church members, and staff members. They contained the crisis as best they could and solidified the congregation's footing for the long recovery ahead.

The Communication Challenge

Leading a congregation out of the initial chaos of a crisis demands a cool head, a warm heart, and a built-in bias for action. Communication has special importance in this regard.

The Benefits of Communication

Why communicate? It sounds like a silly question since we recognize the importance of crisis communication intuitively. Still, it helps to remind ourselves precisely why it's so valuable. Consider these ten benefits of effective communication:

1. Fills the void of the unknown, thus reducing people's anxiety
2. Squelches rumors
3. Shows that leaders are aware of the situation, are taking it seriously, and are working to contain and resolve it
4. Reinforces congregational mission, vision, and values
5. Strengthens a congregation's sense of community
6. Bolsters morale
7. Empowers people by helping them understand how they can be part of the solution

8. Bears witness to the congregation's faith in God
9. Surfaces additional information for crisis response because it runs two ways
10. Facilitates healing by giving people an avenue to express their grief

We simply cannot overstate the importance of communication. In crisis, people suffer from confusion and uncertainty. They experience loss. They need timely, accurate information. They need clear instructions. They also need reminders of the vision, values, and hope that will anchor them in the storm. Leaders provide this kind of communication.

Crisis Communication: A Collaborative Process

Assuming that you act on the advice given earlier in the chapter about building a team to orchestrate the congregation's crisis response, you will want to activate the group as quickly as possible and put crisis communication high on the group's tactical agenda. You won't have long before it becomes essential to address those who are concerned, which makes it more likely that they can cooperate with the effort to contain the crisis.

Our audiences. Working in tandem with others, make a list of those who need to hear from you. Because you may need to customize your message to fit your audiences, you will want to think holistically and begin with those most affected by the crisis. Identify key groups of leaders–staff, boards, committees, organizations, ministry teams. Expand your thinking further to include key segments of the congregation (age groups, for instance).

Be mindful, as well, of your congregation's relationships with those outside the church. Are there neighbors, service providers, public officials, related congregations, or denominational and other church-related organizations with an interest in what's going on? Include them on your list. Will news media come into play? You will definitely want to think about how best to handle communication with them.

Our message. Communication during the crisis containment stage poses some unique challenges. Emotions run high, information is incomplete, and conditions are in flux. What do we say?

For sure, we need to say something. Nature abhors a vacuum. Absent reliable information, people will make things up, rumors will fly, and conditions will deteriorate.

In the fall of 2006, Taco Bell was forced to close several of its restaurants after dozens of people in the Northeastern United States became sick from E. coli–contaminated lettuce. Taco Bell's crisis management teams acted swiftly to protect public health interests and trace the problem to its source. Unfortunately, they handled the communication task poorly, failing to provide the public with adequate information. Speculation turned what was actually a geographically isolated problem into a national scare. Two weeks into the crisis, frustrated news people still waited for answers to some of their basic questions.[11]

We dare not wait until we have complete information before going public. To avoid a situation like the one Taco Bell helped to create, we need to move quickly to tell people what we know, when we knew it, and what we plan to do about it. Avoiding the temptation to speculate where we lack hard facts, we need to acknowledge what we don't know yet and explain the steps we're taking to get to the bottom of things. As details come in, we need to provide communication updates.

In my experience through the years, people appreciate candor almost as much as they appreciate facts. They will exercise patience and understanding if they see leaders as engaged, caring, and diligent about getting facts and marshaling resources to address the problem. Their attitude becomes even more positive if the message includes a call to action.

During the first hours and days after our youth group's bus accident, those of us involved in communication processes provided continuous updates to the church, the community, and our global audience. We also relayed information about the ways people could participate in caring response. Some of our members, and even a few people beyond the church, cooked up their own ideas for action. We reported these developments and facilitated member participation in these initiatives when possible. This led to such things as group prayer events; a prayer wall in a main corridor of the church that was covered from floor to ceiling with cards, letters, e-mails, and other tokens of love; a Facebook page dedicated to victims, their families, and the church as a whole; and a bus accident fund.

It's important to note that our message needs to be about more than the facts. Our message needs to speak to the perceptions, feelings, aspirations, and behaviors of our audience as well. Our message is about the following:

- *Facts.* We tell the truth, as best we know it. We refuse to minimize, blame, or speculate. We get all the bad news out as we get it.
- *Perceptions.* We provide perspective by framing the crisis in a way that's consistent with our faith in God and our love for one another.
- *Feelings.* We pay attention to the tone of our communication. We express empathy, grief, and confidence. If we've made mistakes, we acknowledge this and express remorse. We give people permission to experience their own feelings too.
- *Aspirations.* We encourage positive expectations and genuine hope by pointing people toward a desirable vision of the future.
- *Behaviors.* We talk honestly about actions that are helpful and actions that aren't helpful.

Our mode. Communication in the midst of crisis has become easier *and* more complicated as a result of ongoing developments in the area of social media. When it comes to thinking through avenues, or modes, of communication, we do well to make the most of all the ones available to us.

When I think back to the hours and days immediately following the bus accident, I can rattle off several modes of communication we used:

- In our two worship services on July 12, we communicated face-to-face with all Sunday-morning attenders, and we continued to meet for worship and prayer as the days and weeks went by.
- We communicated by telephone with those who had been on the bus and with good Samaritans, like the pastor of FBC, Meridian, Mississippi.
- We interacted with the public through local and national news media (television and print).
- We made it possible for our people to visit our Web site for updates.
- We interacted with people by e-mail and used blasts to keep people up to date.
- Facebook became an extremely important source of ongoing interaction among people worldwide.
- Texting provided an additional source of instant communication. Our youth made particularly significant use of it.

I felt great appreciation toward our youth for how tightly networked they were. On Monday morning, we formalized plans for a gathering of those who had been on the bus and were back in town. We didn't have much time for getting the word out, but we thought it was important to get everyone back together as soon as possible to facilitate the healing process and experience the strength of fellowship and prayer. We invited a therapist from the community to help facilitate the meeting. We invited parents to participate too, and wanted youth who hadn't been on the trip to show up at the end of our debriefing experience so they could reconnect with their friends. Getting the word out proved extremely simple: our youth secretary made phone calls, and our youth used their phones to call and text one another. Some even got word through Facebook. In the days that followed, we were able to move rapidly to put gatherings together because of these capabilities.

Two-way communication. It's worth noting that two-way communication makes a big difference. In the immediate aftermath of a crisis-precipitating event, people have thoughts, feelings, needs, ideas, and questions. Providing them with ways to express themselves is helpful to them *and* to the leaders who are managing things. Whether by means of question and answer sessions or well-advertised telephone numbers and e-mail addresses, people need to know that they can get through to someone who's caring, knowledgeable, and responsive.

The pastor as messenger-in-chief. During his eight years as president of the University of Wyoming (1997–2005), Philip Dubois led that institution through numerous crises, including two that drew national and international media attention: the vicious murder of gay UW student Matthew Shepard in October 1998 and the deaths of eight members of the men's cross-country and track teams in an automobile accident on September 16, 2001. In a 2003 forum on leadership, Dubois reflected on some of the lessons that had emerged from his experience as a crisis leader. One lesson resonated with many of us: "In times of severe crisis, the President's voice matters, and it may be the only one that does." While elaborating on his assertion, he added that

> in cases of severe crisis, members of the community will look to [the president] for words of comfort and even inspiration. For those moments in time, the President's values are the institution's values, and they cannot be conveyed with passion and meaning in a press release or by a press spokesperson.[12]

Applied to congregational life, this lesson suggests that, in a time of crisis, the executive and spiritual leader of the church, the pastor (or, in the absence of the pastor, one other key leader) serves as what might be called the messenger-in-chief. The messenger-in-chief captures the meaning of the moment in words, applies the balm of compassion, and inspires an uncommon commitment to the mission, vision, and values of the congregation. As noted earlier in the chapter, this responsibility can't be fully realized in absentia. Unless logistically impossible, the messenger-in-chief must deliver messages personally and openly. People need to see sincerity in the messenger's eyes. They need to hear compassion in the messenger's voice. They need to experience the tone as well as the content of what the messenger has to say. The pastor defines reality, comforts all who mourn, and points toward a horizon of hope beyond the crisis.

Over the course of a congregational crisis, from onset to resolution, more than one person is likely to play an important communication role on behalf of the church, though it is wise to have a designated crisis communication coordinator as point person who is managing the process and ensuring that the church is speaking with one voice. This point person may or may not be the pastor, depending on any number of factors—the size of the church, the nature of the crisis, the availability of people with special expertise, the degree to which the church is organized in advance for crisis response, the pastor's preferences and skill set, and so on.

The fact remains that as messenger-in-chief, the pastor has a communication-related role to play that is unique to the position. At no time does this unique role matter more intensely than at the earliest edge of a crisis.

It mattered to the members of Wedgwood Baptist Church that Pastor Meredith stood in the media glare on the night of the shootings (and repeatedly in the days following), offering information and insight and declaring, "We will not give an inch to the darkness!" It mattered to them that on the very next Sunday, in the same room where the shootings had occurred, he could address the question, "Where Was God?" His ongoing voice at funerals and special gatherings and in the media became a metronome of realism, resilience, and hope.

Handling the News Media

Many congregational crises happen below the radar of the news media. These congregations can face their difficulties without the added challenges of an onlooking world. This was the case for Crosspointe Meadows Church in Novi, Michigan. In 2008 they found themselves caught in the undertow of a region-wide economic crisis. Virtually every organization in the region had to wrestle with urgent, difficult issues. Nothing about Crosspointe Meadows's problems distinguished it or drew media attention.

You, on the other hand, may find yourself dealing with the media. In that case, here are some rules of thumb to go by.

Cultivate a good relationship under normal circumstances. Some of the resources I evaluated during my research had a negative predisposition toward the media. This can become a self-fulfilling prophesy, setting us up to expect the worst of each other and get the worst from each other. In my experience, it's healthier to develop a mutually respectful relationship, while also understanding how the interests of the media compare and contrast with the interests of the church. Their objective isn't to facilitate your church's mission; their objective is to sell news. Accepting this fact allows you to look for synergies between your interests and theirs, such as providing them with interesting stories, being sensitive to their deadlines, helping them get their facts right, and expressing appreciation to them when you find opportunities to do so.

Be prepared for a rush of phone calls when word of the crisis gets out. Late-breaking news is the bread and butter of the media. As soon as they learn of a newsworthy development, they can be counted on to jump on the story. From your side of things, this may not be convenient. It adds another layer of complexity to a situation that may already feel overwhelming. It detracts from other activity that you may have put high on your agenda. Nevertheless, you are wise to prepare yourself for the media and allow time to address their questions. If someone other than you has been appointed as primary spokesperson then politely point the media to that spokesperson for further information.

Be responsive. Media outlets work on deadlines. Keep this in mind when responding. If you can't talk immediately, ask them what deadline they're working on and promise to get back to them. Then by all means, follow through on your promise.

"Frame the story" and represent your point of view. One reason to respond quickly to the media is that you want to get in front of the story and provide a constructive perspective for understanding what's happened. In the aftermath of Wedgwood's trauma with a gunman, Pastor Meredith wanted to make sure that the story didn't devolve into an issue of gun control, mental illness, or security processes. He framed the situation in spiritual terms—as something that happens in a spiritually fractured world—and signaled that the church would respond with resilience and grace.

Be accurate, candid. Generally speaking, the truth will come out, one way or another. The question is: Will your organization be the one to make the facts known, or will the facts surface despite you? It's better to serve as the original and best source of information and the original interpreter of that information. This will include expressions of sympathy for those impacted by the crisis and an honest acceptance of responsibility. On October 27, 2010, a student videographer at the University of Notre Dame was killed when a hydraulic lift he was on toppled over while he was filming football practice. The president of the university, the Rev. John Jenkins, wasted no time doing a preliminary investigation of what had happened. On November 5, he sent an e-mail to students, faculty, staff, and alumni saying that the school was responsible for the student's death because it failed to protect him.[13] It is wise in crises that pose potential liability issues to have legal counsel. In the final analysis, however, your leadership team will want to be guided by its values and not just by its self-protective instincts.

Remember that tone matters as much as content. Whoever stands before the public in the name of the church will become the public face of the congregation. They will set the tone that the public sees. It is important to convey character, compassion, and confidence.

Use the right spokesperson and speak with a single voice. If you've ever watched a public-sector news conference related to a crisis, you will notice that it usually begins with a lead spokesperson who provides an initial overview of the situation and then turns things over to one or more specialists who can provide more detailed information related to their knowledge of the situation or their special expertise. Depending on the nature of your crisis, you may have people you want to call on to supply a more in-depth analysis.

By all means, speak with a single voice. The best way to do this is to have a designated spokesperson and to channel all media interaction through them. You may want to have a backup spokesperson as well, who can step in should your primary spokesperson not be available. Whoever serves as spokesperson needs to be kept in the information loop and to work closely with the rest of the crisis action team as the story unfolds. The better prepared they are to answer potential questions and to shape the tone and content of the congregation's message, the better the media and the public will respond to the crisis.

Understand that in a networked world like ours, communication with anyone has potential to become communication with everyone. Mention has already been made of the value of targeted communication. Each of our audiences has its own interests and needs. This will affect the content and the modes of our communication. Having said this, it's wise to assume that anything you communicate to one audience will find its way to other audiences. Apart from deliberations and decisions that belong within the boundaries of confidentiality (e.g., personnel matters or the identity of victims prior to notification of family), openness with all is generally the best policy. You will want to make sure that public notice doesn't get ahead of news that special audiences need to know first. It's not mere happenstance that President Jenkins of Notre Dame chose e-mail as his avenue of communication when responding publicly to the tragic death of the student videographer.

Think opportunistically. See the media as a potential ally for communication purposes. Media coverage will assist your effort to communicate with members. It can alert the public to ways they can support the congregation. It gives you a chance to express your congregation's mission, vision, and values. It increases the possibility that your church will be remembered not for the crisis, but for how it responded to the crisis.[14]

Leading a Congregation at the Outset of Crisis

The first characteristic shared by all congregations in crisis is that, to one degree or another, crises catch the congregation off guard and throw it into a state of confusion. Crises create chaos. Effective leaders, with cool heads, warm hearts, and a built-in bias for action, see themselves as instruments of God to restore sanity and order to the situation. Some of them do this under the glare of the media spotlight while others do so without public scrutiny. Either way, leadership at the outset of crisis helps stabilize the situation and set the congregation on the road to recovery.

Reflection Questions

Reflect personally on the following questions. If you are using this book with a study group, share your perspectives with each other. If you aren't currently experiencing a congregational crisis, think of a crisis your congregation has experienced or might experience and project yourself into that situation when reflecting on the questions.

- Which is easier for you: a cool head, a warm heart, or a built-in bias for action? Which is harder for you? What can you do to make sure that all three are firmly in play in the leadership of the church?

- Who needs to be at the leadership or management table as you respond to crisis (what authority, influence, skills, and experience do you need at your disposal)?
- What could you do to improve communication right now? Is there an audience you could better serve? Is there information you need to share? Is there input or feedback you need to get? Are there communication modes you might use more?

Congregations in Focus

University Baptist Church, Waco, Texas

Celebration can turn to tragedy in an instant.

On Sunday morning, October 30, 2005, around 850 people crowded into the sanctuary of Waco's University Baptist Church (UBC). Almost two hundred of them were guests who had come to town for Baylor University's homecoming weekend.

After greetings, announcements, and some early worship singing, teaching Pastor Kyle Lake stepped into the baptistery to baptize a young woman. He reached out to adjust a microphone on a floor stand in front of the baptistery and immediately felt a surge of electricity. He cried for help and collapsed in the water. A member of the worship band quickly unplugged the microphone cable, and others rushed into the water to pull him out. The one getting set to be baptized was standing at the edge of the water, shocked but unhurt.

In the urgency of the next moments, physicians in the congregation hurried to the area behind the baptistery to treat Kyle, while attendees reacted in a variety of ways, from quiet concern to urgent praying. Community pastor Ben Dudley stepped into the confusion, having been occupied until then outside the sanctuary. A seasoned pastor in attendance that morning prompted the young Pastor Dudley to explain the situation and give instructions for exiting the building. An ambulance arrived and carried Kyle to Hillcrest Baptist Medical Center, where he was pronounced dead at 11:30 a.m.

How does a congregation handle things when death steals its gifted young pastor? Kyle, though only thirty-three years old at the time of his death, had already made a mark in and beyond his congregation.

Author of two books, *Understanding God's Will: How to Hack the Equation without Formulas* and *(RE)Understanding Prayer: A Fresh Approach to Conversation with God,*[1] Kyle was known for his ability to reach out to younger audiences, such as the college-age crowd. He had surfaced as a promising young leader in the Emerging Church movement. Among UBCers, he was known as a life-embracing, fun-loving, relationship-building person. He left behind his wife, Jennifer, and three young children, Avery, Sutton, and Jude.

News of his death spread quickly. Within minutes local news stations began calling for interviews. Ben reached out for advice to one of those involved with the church since its inception—assistant professor of communication studies, Dr. Blair Browning. Not only did Browning offer suggestions for how to handle things that afternoon, he also agreed subsequently to serve on an open-ended basis as media coordinator. He became an integral part of the church leadership team's ongoing response to the crisis and the point person for internal communication and interactions with news organizations. An initial interview at the church included an official statement and the announcement that the congregation would gather that evening at Waco's First Baptist Church (FBC) for a remembrance of Kyle, to be preceded by a formal press conference.

FBC's hospitality on the night of the tragedy was just the beginning of gracious support from those beyond the church. Baylor University and its theological school, Truett Baptist Theological Seminary, made campus space available on Sundays and Wednesdays in the early weeks after the tragedy. Churches took up offerings, which made it possible to set up a scholarship fund for the Lake children. One church supplied meals to the staff three times a week for a full month. Baylor faculty and staff lent their expertise in a variety of ways, at no charge. People from around the world learned of the accident and reached out with love and prayers.

This generosity of support figured into the leadership team's decision about what to do concerning its worship leadership needs. Gideon Tsang, one of the pastors of an innovative church plant in Austin, Texas—one hundred miles away—agreed to travel back and forth each Sunday in the role of interim teaching pastor. Others filled in on occasion.

Other important decisions had to be made as well. The church building itself became an issue, initially because police investigators and facility inspectors barred its use, and then because the trauma of Kyle's death had cast a pall over it. The leadership team decided to guide the congregation through a period of grief before returning, which also provided a window of opportunity for remodeling. The facility, purchased from another congregation, had years of wear and tear. Leaders wanted to alter the sanctuary in the aftermath of Kyle's death. Funding for the work came readily from those in and beyond the church. In the meantime, UBC gathered at alternate locations, first on the Baylor campus and then at the Hippodrome Theater, just off the campus. One of the serendipitous by-products of this disruption was a resurgence of the kind of fluid communication and congregational life that characterized the church at its inception in 1995.

Central to UBC's recovery from crisis was the grief process. They had suffered a double loss: the loss of a friend and the loss of their vision leader. On the Sunday night of Kyle's death, the stunned congregation gathered in FBC's sanctuary, surrounded by a host of others. Ben Dudley told the UBC congregation that night that they would move forward as a church: "I don't know how, when, why, where, or what's going to happen, but we will continue as a church in the community because that is what Kyle would have wanted."

Tuesday's funeral, again at FBC with a graveside service following, provided a memorable time to celebrate Kyle's life, grieve, and look to God for grace. Dr. Burt Burleson, a friend of Kyle's and at the time a fellow pastor in the community, drew words from Kyle's sermon notes for October 30 to inspire and encourage.

> Live. And live well . . . BREATHE. Breathe in and breathe deeply . . . Be PRESENT. Do not be past. Do not be future. Be now . . . Feel the SATISFACTION of a job well done . . . If you've recently experienced loss, then GRIEVE. And Grieve well . . . At the table with friends and family, LAUGH . . . And TASTE. Taste every ounce of flavor. Taste every ounce of friendship. Taste every ounce of Life. Because-it-is-most-definitely-a-Gift.

These words continue to encourage and inspire the congregation. The leadership team acted deliberately to promote healthy grieving. A team of counselors from Baylor University facilitated the process at Wednesday night gatherings for several weeks following the accident. Simultaneously, the homes of UBCers became informal settings of love and mutual support. At the one-year anniversary of Kyle's death, the church held a special commemoration of his life.

Grieving was complicated by the very public and traumatic nature of Kyle's death and the legal issues that followed. In May 2006, Kyle's family filed a wrongful death lawsuit against the electrical company that had installed the baptistery, ultimately settling the case at the end of November 2006. Though the church itself wasn't accused in the lawsuit, its involvement required legal representation, and ongoing developments kept wounds fresh. Kyle's wife and children remained active in the church throughout this time.

UBC's recovery from crisis can be marked in stages and was tied in some ways to the rhythms of university life, given that at the time of the accident 65–70 percent of the church's participants were college students. An intense, initial stage of grief lasted through the balance of the 2005 fall semester. Staff began officing at the church again in the early days of 2006. Contractors completed renovations during the following summer, and the church community returned to the church's campus in time for the fall semester. The leadership team waited a full year before hiring a second community pastor to handle ministry management needs, and it waited two years to name a new teaching pastor, Josh Carney.

Josh and the rest of the leadership team have found ways to preserve Kyle's legacy while helping the church look forward with missional purpose. The experience has provided sobering insight into the challenges of congregational polity. Members of the leadership team readily acknowledge that they learned hard lessons about congregational communication and decision making. The church's intimate encounter with death and suffering also deepened its commitment to an authentic community and sensitized it to the pain of other congregations that experience trauma.

Before Kyle's death, the church had begun to shift its ministry focus beyond the college community. This shift stalled but is being reasserted again, with greater attention to God's missional calling into the city, the surrounding region, and the world. Illustrative of this are its partnership with a neighboring middle school and its involvements in Kenya through the One Laptop per Child program and an economic development project for impoverished Kenyans.

Grateful for Kyle Lake's legacy, University Baptist Church has moved forward. It has drawn strength from God through suffering and found fresh ways to fulfill its calling. At the same time, it remains committed to the spirit behind Kyle's best known benediction: "Love God, Embrace Beauty, and Live Life to the Fullest."[2]

5

Managing the Mess

Putting the Congregation on the Road to Recovery

A congregational crisis doesn't end when the dust settles. In some ways, it has just begun.

When the dust settled at University Baptist Church in Waco, Texas, after Kyle Lake's sudden death, the crisis still required the church to process congregation-wide trauma and grief and deal with a vacuum of pastoral leadership.

At a church in the Southeast that prefers to remain anonymous, financial problems didn't suddenly evaporate when the initial shock of crisis died down. The church treasurer had siphoned off building fund assets and then committed suicide when his embezzlement was discovered. The church had to deal with whether it could complete the project, how it would meet its ongoing financial obligations, and what to do about pastoral and legal issues related to the treasurer's family.

In 2007, the Washington State Department of Transportation provoked a crisis for Lake Washington Christian Church in Kirkland, Washington, when it informed them of its intentions to claim their property for freeway expansion. This notice led to two years of legal wrangling. The shock of the announcement wore off quickly while the crisis lingered.

When it turned out that cracks in the sanctuary floor had resulted from serious leaks in its fifty-year-old underground heating pipes, New Horizon Christian Church in Akron, Ohio, went into a state of high alert. The shock of discovery didn't last long; but it took months to take care of the situation.

Each of these stories illustrates that crisis leadership is a long-distance run, not a sprint. The seriousness of these crises varied widely. The extent of the disruptions did too. The crises brought differences in the scale of the crisis, the number of people affected, the nature of the damage, the duration of the disruptions, and the level of peril to the ongoing work of the church. Nevertheless, in every one of these cases, leaders responded faithfully over an extended period of time and shepherded their congregations through the difficulties.

This chapter looks more closely at the longer journey of crisis response. Picking up where the previous chapter ended, it focuses on the challenges of crisis leadership during the days, weeks, or even months when crisis is at its highest. What do you do once you've absorbed the initial blow of a crisis? You turn your attention toward congregational recovery. Leading during this stage of crisis response brings a distinct set of strategic, logistical, and pastoral activities into play.

Orchestrate the Recovery Process

One of your principle roles during this stage of a crisis is to orchestrate the recovery process. Like conductors of a choral or instrumental performance, crisis leaders bring the right players to the stage, make sure they all know their parts, and keep them moving in harmony and at the right tempo toward a new normal that honors God.

Clarify the Goal of Crisis Response

In overall terms, what does an effective recovery from crisis look like? What is the goal of crisis response? Since your church is on a journey toward its full potential in Christ, the goal of crisis response is to resolve the consequences of the crisis into a new normal that is further along in that direction. Your goal isn't just to settle things down and get back to business as usual. Your goal isn't merely to dig yourself out of a hole or restore things to their previous condition or get over the emotional trauma of what has taken place. Your goal is to be more the congregation God wants you to be at the end of the process than you were at the outset. You want God to use the crisis as an occasion for the missional development of your church.

Use Key Management Strategies to Orchestrate Congregational Recovery

Once you have focused on this as your goal, you have something toward which to aim as you orchestrate recovery. Then it's time to orchestrate. This involves the use of basic project management techniques:[1]

- define objectives
- build a team
- plan the work

- work the plan
- monitor progress
- achieve the objectives
- close down the project (this will be the focus of the next chapter)

Define Objectives

Take time to clarify your crisis recovery objectives as soon as you can. It's tempting to skip this step, to jump into crisis response with a focus on immediate needs to the neglect of eventual outcomes. Skipping this crucial step brings more than one problem.

For one thing, you can end up doing things that don't contribute to crisis resolution. You can actually complicate the recovery process instead. Consider, for instance, the temptation to help people in crisis in a way that develops dependency rather than resiliency. Animated by a compassionate impulse, we rush into action. Victims' immediate needs are met (as is our urge to feel needed). Then compassion fatigue sets in. We withdraw, leaving those we've cared for unprepared to deal with their problems. Inevitably, they feel abandoned. Without thoughtful objectives, gut instincts take over and we get caught up in the moment and become negligent of long-term consequences.

On another note, without clear objectives you lack a solid basis for knowing when your crisis has reached resolution. You then run the risk of declaring the crisis over too soon or long after it has actually ended. When the members of New Life Church in Colorado Springs, Colorado, began working with counselors to process the trauma of a gunman's attack in December 2007, congregational leaders clearly recognized that emotional wounds from the previous year's crisis had not fully healed. Conversations kept turning back to founding pastor Ted Haggard and the scandal that led to his departure in November 2006. The discovery of this unresolved grief prompted congregational leaders to be much more intentional about dealing with the emotional trauma of the armed intruder. They know now that it would have been helpful in the aftermath of Haggard's resignation to establish clear objectives and a set of criteria for evaluating progress related to the psychological aftereffects of the first crisis on members.

Finally, without clear objectives you will have trouble distinguishing between crisis concerns and continuing concerns. A *crisis concern* is an issue that the congregation must resolve in order to move beyond the crisis. A *continuing concern*, though it still matters interpersonally and even strategically, doesn't disrupt the congregation's ability to get past the crisis and move on. First Baptist Shreveport's bus accident left some of those on the bus with serious injuries. They had to deal with surgery, long-term rehabilitation, and mounting medical expenses. At what point, if any, did these issues cross the threshold from crisis concern to continuing concern? Could First Baptist Shreveport consider its crisis resolved prior to the resolution of these medical matters? These are the kinds of questions that need to be addressed when developing plans for crisis recovery. Thoughtful objectives provide you with clear, attainable, and measurable criteria for determining where you are in the crisis recovery process.

Your ability to orchestrate the recovery begins with clarity of direction. You need to know the end toward which the process is aimed. Take time at the outset to zero in on the outcomes you seek. Stay focused on strategic objectives as they relate to the crisis itself. Make sure the objectives you set meet the standard for effective objectives:

- *They are clearly defined.* They give you a solid sense of direction.
- *They are decisive.* They establish how you'll know you've arrived.
- *They are attainable.* It's essential to be realistic about what's possible.

Build a Team

Your first objective, if you haven't done so already, is to activate a crisis management team. This team will work with you to clarify the other objectives, develop action plans, and oversee the crisis recovery process. This team will include key congregational decision makers, members with project management skills and special expertise related to your particular crisis, and maybe even outside support people, if needed.

Almost inevitably, people step forward when crisis strikes and find ways to be helpful. They may step forward because of servant instincts. They may step forward because of their formal role of leadership in the church. They may show up because you called on them. Very seldom will you start from scratch when it comes to mobilizing a team for the longer-term process of crisis recovery. Some of those who help at the outset of crisis will become core members of the team.

The key now is to be intentional about creating a formal team recognized by the church as the nerve center of the recovery effort. This team will plan and oversee the work. Individual members of the team will also coordinate discrete aspects of the work and mobilize task groups, in some cases, to help. The team will need to meet regularly to coordinate the effort.

University Baptist Church of Waco leaned on its preexisting church leadership team to guide its recovery process after Kyle Lake's death. Composed of staff members, key ministry leaders, and their spouses, this group met regularly to strategize, make assignments, and monitor developments. The group also called on outside expertise and support, especially benefitting from Baylor University faculty in the areas of communication and counseling.

After First Baptist Shreveport's bus accident in July 2009, I could not have done by myself what needed doing. Not only was there *too much* to do, but the situation called for managerial strengths and expertise I do not have. Big picture? Yes. Strategic direction and oversight? Not a problem.

Catalytic initiative? One of my strong suits. Details and routine medical and legal expertise? Not so much.

That's where volunteer leaders like Susie Holton proved so valuable. She became resource central for communicating with church members, organizing volunteers, and collecting contributions. She functioned like a full-time, unpaid staff person for the next four weeks, tending to an untold number of details. She was an integral member of the crisis recovery team that met and monitored progress.

Skill set is a critical variable in the leadership/management equation. Also critical is one's availability. Gene Hendrix, the Minister of Christian Formation and Administration, had the necessary skills to handle the management side of our caring response to the crisis; but he had so many other things to do that it would have been irresponsible to ask him to orchestrate this himself. He participated as a member of the crisis response team, but he was glad to have a larger team to oversee the process.

Building a team is objective number one. When doing so, keep these things in mind:

- Create a team with complementary strengths.
- Clarify objectives, tasks, and assignments up front.
- Meet regularly to coordinate the effort, solve problems, and keep things moving in the right direction.
- Be sure to empower those on the team to take initiative within the parameters of their assignment and authority. (In other words, formally authorize them, and don't micromanage!)
- Make sure they have access to the resources they need to do what they've been asked to do.
- Recognize people for the contributions they make to the process.

No matter how big or small the church, a crisis creates a potentially mind-boggling number of moving parts. Leaders must collaborate to address the needs of the hour and the long-term interests of the church.

Plan the Work

Once you've formed the crisis management team, develop your recovery plan. Planning starts with the objectives and works backward to clarify the activity that will get you to the outcomes you seek. What tasks need doing? Who are the most qualified individuals or groups to accomplish each task? How much time do you think each task will take? How will you sequence the tasks?

One of the issues that may come into play as you plan is whether to use volunteers or professionals to do the recovery work. Will you hire a contractor, an accountant, an attorney, a team of counselors; or will you lean on the volunteer services of your members? There is not one right answer. Every church must make this decision for itself.

When trustees at New Horizon Christian Church in Akron, Ohio, discovered heating pipe leaks in the slab floor of their sanctuary in April 2008, they mobilized skilled members and other volunteers to deal with the problem. The do-it-ourselves nature of the work didn't create a problem in terms of quality, given the skill level of the members involved, but it did lead to project delays related to people's work schedules. Initially conceived as a summer project, the congregation didn't return to the sanctuary until Advent, and replacement pews didn't get installed until the following spring. Nonetheless, the project involved a lot of members and strengthened the esprit de corps of the congregation.

Congregational United Church of Christ (CUCC) in Punta Gorda, Florida, went the professional route to deal with damage to its building after Hurricane Charley. Insurance coverage and other available funds took care of repair and renovation costs. The entire church building was actually reroofed on a single Saturday, one week after the hurricane.

Here are a few considerations to guide you as you decide which way to go. Go the volunteer route when any or all of the following apply:

- Quality matters less than member involvement.
- You have time flexibility.
- Money is an issue.

Go the professional route when any or all of the following apply:

- You don't want to leave quality to chance.
- You face time constraints.
- You can afford to pay for professional services, or those services are being offered free of charge or at a greatly reduced price.

In many situations, crisis response will call for a combination of the two. Fortunate is the congregational leader who has skilled professionals in the church who can lend their expertise to the situation. In the aftermath of our bus accident, our church benefitted from the expertise of several members, including an attorney, a television reporter, a newspaper editor, a clinical social worker, two private counselors, and more than one physician. They offered their expertise out of love for the church, never giving a thought to billing us.

A caveat needs to be added. Just because you have professionals in the church doesn't mean that you can or will lean on them. Some, in fact, make it a policy not to establish contractual relationships with their church or to volunteer their professional services because of the risks to the relationship or perceptions of favoritism (related to the fact that there are other members with the same credentials). Again, every situation is unique. There is no right or wrong answer. You have to exercise your judgment and accept the consequences, whether good or bad.

Collaborative leadership isn't limited to the congregation's membership. Effective leaders take the time to build relationships in the community and acquaint themselves with the expertise of people in the community. Having a positive relationship with the volunteer fire department served Sandy Run Baptist Church in Hampton, South Carolina, well when the fire broke out in the sanctuary. One of the church's deacons was actually the leader of the firefighting team that responded within minutes when the fire alarm sounded.

Having relationships with go-to people in such fields as medicine, law, insurance, media, construction, and mental health comes in handy when crises come. And don't underplay the significance of collegiality with others in the faith community. More than one of the leaders I interviewed expressed gratitude to fellow pastors, denominational executives, and members from other congregations for the assistance they offered in the process of recovering from crisis. At First Baptist Shreveport we were graced by many expressions of kindness. Shreveport's Broadmoor Baptist Church, for instance, provided equipment and technical support so we could provide a live online broadcast of the funeral for Maggie Lee Henson. We even benefitted from the kindness of a church two hundred miles away that provided props for our Vacation Bible School and sent two members to deliver them.

Work the Plan

The plan is only as good as its actual execution; so once you have a plan, put it into motion. Every act in the direction of crisis resolution lifts the spirits of those who have been unsettled by the crisis, including you and your team. People regain control of their lives. They see circumstances stabilizing. They feel less overwhelmed and more hopeful. A sense of order replaces chaos.

In the aftermath of First Baptist Shreveport's bus accident, we had objectives and action plans related to pastoral care issues, operational issues, insurance issues, legal issues, and communications issues. We forged a team of skilled and attentive people who took on assignments related to each issue. Working together and separately, we began chipping away at our challenge. The congregation was reassured to know that details were being tended to and that they could help in specific ways. They couldn't do much about medical and legal matters—these called for special expertise and access to sometimes confidential information. They could, however, participate in the congregation's caring response to bus accident victims and their families. They could rally together in worship and prayer. They could give their best to the ongoing ministries of the church—like the Vacation

Bible School that began one week after the bus accident. Thoughtful planning gave us a way to mobilize members and channel in a constructive way their pent-up desire to help.

Monitor Progress

A crisis, by its very nature, is a moving target. It creates a chain reaction of consequences, some of them predictable, some of them not. Furthermore, a congregation's response to crisis introduces new dynamics into the situation, solving problems even as it surfaces new ones. As crisis leaders, you and the rest of the crisis management team will have reason to meet regularly for updates about how things are going. Your plans will evolve as new information presents itself and circumstances change.

Anyone who has led an organization, even for a few months, knows that making assignments and completing assignments are two different things. Crisis recovery depends on leaders who regularly ask

- are all planned tasks under way?
- are all tasks on schedule, or have some hit obstacles?
- are we staying current with communication to the congregation and others with natural interests in what's going on?
- are we keeping a written record of decisions and developments for later review?

As for holding the recovery process to a schedule, some aspects of this will be easier than others. You can place town hall meetings and prayer events on the calendar. You can put yourself on the clock when gathering information for decision making. You can target completion dates for construction work and repairs. However, it's more difficult to anticipate the time it will take to resolve legal or medical matters. The time it takes for emotional recovery from trauma also varies widely from person to person.

Create completion dates for aspects of the recovery over which you have control and be persistent to encourage progress where friendly pressure will keep things moving forward. At the same time, exercise patience about things over which you have little or no control, and allow plenty of time and opportunity for people to recover emotionally. Getting over your crisis is less important than getting your crisis recovery right.

By all means keep the lines of communication open. Those with an interest in your crisis and crisis recovery, whether church members or otherwise, need to be kept apprised of progress, setbacks, and changes of plan.

Expect Complications

You might as well prepare yourself for complications. As the Scottish poet Robert Burns observed, "The best laid plans of mice and men often go awry."[2]

Expect aftershocks. On the afternoon of March 11, 2011, an earthquake registering 9.0 on the Richter scale shook northern Japan, unleashing waves of disaster that destroyed entire communities and cost tens of thousands of people their lives. Japan actually experienced multiple earthquakes immediately prior to the "big one." It also experienced dozens of aftershocks, many of which registered 6.0 or higher on the Richter scale. The earthquakes were devastating. Then the tragedy grew exponentially worse because of a tsunami caused by the quake, with waves up to one hundred feet high racing inland at five hundred miles per hour. As if this weren't devastating enough, nuclear danger presented itself when nuclear power plant reactors became damaged.

The Japanese disaster of 2011 was an extraordinary event of vast proportions, but it serves to illustrate that crisis containment and resolution are often complicated by the ripple effects of the initial crisis. Don't be surprised or discouraged if this happens. Remind yourself and others that this is normal. Put your crisis leadership skills into play with each new development by responding calmly and decisively to draw the situation into the process of crisis recovery.

The leadership team of University Baptist Church of Waco had emotional and complex issues to deal with after Kyle Lake's death. They made decisions about where to meet for worship and prayer. They arranged for teaching leadership in the absence of a teaching pastor. They planned and facilitated processes for the grief work of the congregation. Then came the complication of legal issues associated with the installation of the church's baptistery. This development made the news and introduced a new wave of anxiety into the congregation.

After Ted Haggard's resignation as founding pastor of New Life Church in Colorado Springs, the leadership team took careful steps to deal with immediate and long-term needs. Information continued to emerge about Haggard's indiscretions, creating waves of unwelcome media attention. Participation levels suffered, which forced leaders to make difficult budget adjustments, including staff reductions. The Sunday-morning intrusion of a gunman thirteen months later sent fresh shock waves into the congregation, creating a new set of problems and resurfacing unresolved dimensions of the original crisis. What's more, Haggard didn't disappear. He eventually resurfaced, taking steps to start a new church in the same area. This proved alarming and distracting.

Developments like those at University Baptist and New Life illustrate that complications aren't the exception; they're the rule. Be aware that a crisis sometimes has legs. The initial crisis can be the tip of an unseen iceberg. It can set off a chain of events that continue to challenge the church.

From a leadership standpoint, it's important to remain vigilant and responsive. Depending on the seriousness of follow-up events, you may even have to recreate your recovery plan, which is what leaders at New

Life did when ongoing developments with Ted Haggard intermingled with killings on campus. Accept the simple wisdom of psychiatrist and author Scott Peck, who wrote, "Life is difficult."[3] Accepting this simple wisdom frees you to face the complications that happen and get on with the business of understanding and solving them.

Stay Focused

Anyone who has ever participated in a team sport has heard a coach or fellow player say, "Keep your head in the game." It's a way of challenging us toward peak performance in the face of dangers that would cause our performance to slip. It can come at a crucial time in the course of a game or after a setback or boneheaded play. The admonition translates well into the crisis-recovery circumstances of a church.

Remain True to Mission, Vision, and Values

The more serious the crisis, the greater the likelihood that it will divert the attention of the church from its long-term strategic interests. As a congregational leader, you have responsibility to keep your congregation focused in terms of God's mission, your God-given congregational vision, and the values that guide you.

Under normal circumstances, staying focused is a challenge. Even full-time vision leaders get caught up in the routines and distractions of pastoral ministry and lose sight of the bigger picture. This is even truer of members, who have full-time lives beyond their church involvement. As Bill Hybels puts it, "Vision leaks."

> Something I have to remind myself of constantly is that people in our churches have *real lives*. You heard it here—engagements *other than* church. They have challenging jobs, children to raise, lawns to mow, and bills to pay. Because of all these daily responsibilities, the vision we poured into them on Sunday begins to drain out of them sooner than we think.[4]

If this is true under normal circumstances, imagine how much truer this becomes when, on top of normal distractions, you add the pressures and perplexities of a congregational crisis. When a crisis disrupts the normal life of the church, missional focus becomes especially difficult to sustain. As time goes by and the process of crisis recovery continues, focus becomes increasingly challenging. Congregational and personal energy levels ebb and flow, spirits rise and fall, attention twists and turns, interests shift. Congregational leaders must lead with focus and assertiveness to ensure that the congregation stays on track.

The Ways Congregations Get Taken Off Course

Congregations get taken off course in any number of ways. Sometimes they get caught up in crisis mode and *short-shrift activities that serve their mission.* After the fire that damaged Sandy Run Baptist Church, some members thought the church would have to downsize its Sunday morning Bible study plans. Pastor Paul Reid and others in leadership never seriously considered this alternative. Preserving Sunday morning Bible study for all age groups required the use of the parsonage and the renting of mobile units. This meant additional weekly set ups and break downs and other inconveniences, but leaders remained steadfastly committed to this core ministry of the church. They made sure that it continued through the full duration of the rebuilding process.

Sometimes congregations allow shortsightedness to sidetrack them. *The urgent eclipses the important.* How many churches lose a pastor as a consequence of congregational conflict and then jump right into getting a new pastor instead of resolving the issues that led to his departure? How many congregations deal with damaged property by immediately replacing it rather than using the occasion to rethink what they will build (or whether they will build) in light of their emerging mission? How many congregations deal with budget crises by focusing on budget reductions and staff and program cuts to the exclusion of opportunities for the stewardship development of members?

Budget-cutting fever was precisely the temptation we had to address at Holmeswood Baptist Church in Kansas City in order to open ourselves to the opportunity for spiritual and financial growth that lay hidden in our failed campaign to subscribe the 1997 budget. Our church's defining moment never would have happened had we responded to our crisis with mere belt tightening.

Not only can congregations get sidetracked during a crisis by neglecting core ministries or allowing the urgent to eclipse the important, they can get sidetracked by *losing their hold on core values.* Congregations that value transparency can experience breakdowns in communication between leadership and congregation. Congregations that make missions giving a strategic priority can pull back on their missions giving without serious dialogue about the implications. Congregations that pride themselves on their hospitality can allow their crisis-induced security concerns to make them less welcoming.

Let me mention one other way congregations can get taken off course without focused, assertive leadership. Congregations can get *derailed by members with their own agendas.* I've never known a church in which 100 percent of the members share the same level of enthusiasm for the church's current direction. Inevitably, some members or even groups of members disagree with that direction or have interests of their own that don't dovetail with the congregation's current priorities. A crisis gives these people a chance to question congregational direction or advance their personal causes. After Pastor Kyle Lake's death, the elders of University Baptist Church had to deal with people who, perceiving a vacuum of leadership, began pushing their weight around and trying to insert themselves into the leadership picture. The elders, recognizing the need for order, held town hall meetings to establish parameters in the relationship between the leadership team and the church. They provided clarity about the process by which people could be put forward for leadership consideration.

How to Keep the Congregation on Track

How do you keep a congregation on track? You begin by making sure that your *ongoing leadership team* is present and accounted for. Keeping the congregation on track is not the role of the crisis management team (unless the ongoing leadership team is the group coordinating the crisis recovery effort). The crisis management team serves as a valuable ally in the effort to keep the congregation on track, but the work of keeping the congregation on track ultimately belongs to the ongoing leadership team, beginning with the pastor (unless the church is between pastors). The ongoing leadership team factors the crisis into its considerations, develops strategies reflecting the new situation, and engages the congregation in missionally healthy ways.

Keep Yourself *Focused*

Whether you are the pastor or some other member of the ongoing leadership team, you must first manage yourself if you hope to influence the congregation toward health. You must maintain perspective, manage your emotions, and master your instincts in response to the pressures of crisis. If you can keep yourself on track, you will stand a better chance of keeping the congregation on track, channeling its nervous energy and offsetting its opposite tendencies toward inertia, lethargy, and loss of passion (chapter 10 is devoted to this issue).

Normalize All That Can Be Normalized

Crisis leaders in the corporate world give a lot of attention to what they call business continuity. They develop backup plans to keep their businesses running in the event of unwelcome emergencies and disasters. Their goal is to minimize disruptions and speed the return to normal operations. They understand how important this is to the ongoing success of their enterprises.

Business continuity matters for congregations too. A congregation's ability to reestablish a degree of normality in the aftermath of crisis

- helps the church get its bearings again and stay on mission
- increases congregational morale
- gives witness beyond the church to the church's resilience

Do not read this as an invitation to neglect the opportunities for congregational transformation that lie hidden in the devastations of crisis. We will have a good bit to say about this in chapter 7. Normalizing all that can be normalized is simply a way to reestablish the congregation's footing after a crisis has knocked it down.

Furthermore, do not mistake this as a call to ignore the causes and consequences of a crisis. Normalizing all that can be normalized actually frees up time and energy to devote to crisis recovery. It does this by creating a more stable holding environment within which to problem solve and promote healing.

This commitment to normalizing things accounts for New Life Church's decision to carry on with its plans for baby dedications on the Sunday after Ted Haggard's sudden resignation. It explains why Pastor Paul Reid and Sandy Run Baptist Church's other leaders implemented special plans for Sunday school during sanctuary reconstruction. It's what Pastor Bill Klossner had in mind when he commented that CUCC of Punta Gorda, Florida, "never missed worship in the building" after Hurricane Charley: "Our people could count on being here on Sunday, no matter what was going on at their work and home. It provided something stable, something normal."

Be a Mission/Vision Evangelist

During crisis recovery, people need constant reminders about the congregation's most important commitments. Effective leaders use every means at their disposal to hold these commitments high.

On the Sunday following the deadly intrusion of a gunman at Wedgwood Baptist Church, Pastor Al Meredith's message "Where Was God?" spoke to those traumatized by what had happened. The following Sunday, however, he began a six-week sermon series on the church's purpose. He wanted everyone to stay focused on "why we're here and what God wants us to do."

In addition to his preaching and other conventional communication venues, Pastor Brady Boyd used blogging to keep the congregation focused when violence shattered the peace of New Life Church. Entry after entry signaled to online readers that the mission and vision of the church remained undimmed by difficulty. In one entry he wrote, "When we surrender ourselves to the call and purposes of God, heaven responds with power and strength that literally propels us forward, like a ship charging across the waves."[5]

Affirm Every Sign of Congregational Responsiveness and Health

Don't miss an opportunity to reinforce the spirit of resilience. Take time to notice what people are doing to facilitate congregational recovery. Pay attention to evidence of the missional mind-set at work. Then use pulpit, pen, and personal conversation to call attention to it. Say thank you frequently. Give praise for service beyond the call of duty. Celebrate successes large and small. Even consider how to reward exemplary contributions to recovery, whether with bonuses for staff people or tokens of appreciation for volunteers.

One of the best ways to recognize and reward people for their contributions to congregational health is to show them that you take them seriously. Let them know you want to learn from their experience. Give them a chance to brief you on their discoveries. Act on their input when it proves helpful. At First Baptist Shreveport, one of things we did to honor the good work of people was to let them share their stories of service. We hosted a special meeting for volunteers who had participated on post-bus-accident caring teams and let them share their experiences and perspectives. We also provided platform time during worship for testimonies of faith and hope.

Take Gracious but Firm Corrective Action When Something or Someone Goes Off Course

A congregation, even if it understands its mission, will not automatically sail toward recovery any more than a ship will find its way to its destination simply because it has been launched in the right direction. Someone has to stand at the helm making course corrections along the way. Leaders know better than to think that everything will go smoothly.

Leading toward congregation recovery requires attentiveness. Such leading includes guarding against congregational drift. This could mean noticing seeds of the fortress mentality or attempts to put things on hold when things need to keep moving forward. It could have to do with stepping in when you see people using the crisis to advance their personal agendas or to facilitate gossip and unrest.

Any evidence that the congregation's mission and vision are being ignored or thwarted qualifies for corrective action. Sometimes it can have to do with good but misguided intentions. It can happen when people take initiative without coordinating their plans with those who are trying to manage the crisis. They can get ahead of process. They can duplicate efforts. They can do what someone else needs to be doing. It can be simply organizational drift—missing a deadline, postponing a meeting, contributing sloppy work, majoring on minors, failing to communicate adequately, or doing an inadequate job of training people for the work they're being asked to do. It can have to do with loss of enthusiasm or compassion fatigue.

Congregations get off track in an endless number of ways, some of them accidental, some of them intentional. In wise and loving ways, leaders redirect people and processes when they go off course. Reconnecting them to the church's mission, vision, and values, they harness the energy of the church so that it's moving in the same God-honoring direction.

Look for Missional Opportunity in the Crisis Itself

At the time of First Baptist Shreveport's bus accident, we were involved in a construction project to add dedicated space for our youth. For years our youth had been relegated to the activities center, where they had to accommodate the constant intrusions of other church and community activities. Though we already had secured the funding to complete construction, we were still selling the need for this space to the congregation and seeking financial support for finishing touches.

The bus accident reminded all of us how much our youth mattered to us. It focused all of our loving attention on them and gave us a chance to show our commitment to their wellbeing. Backing the construction project became a tangible way to symbolize our support.

You don't have to look far to see missional opportunity in the midst of crisis. With encouragement from effective leaders, hardship and difficulty have a way of reminding us what matters most. It filters out petty differences and trivial pursuits, rallying us around our core commitments and our love for one another. It heightens our appreciation for the promises and purposes of God. Don't miss the opportunity to benefit from this teachable moment in the life of the church.

University Baptist of Waco's months away from its campus after Kyle Lake's death provided an unexpected opportunity to reassert that the church is not just a place; it's a people. "The church became viral," says current teaching pastor, Josh Carney.

> We used the Internet as an essential means of communication, and existing community groups became exceedingly valuable for grief work, mutual support, and discipleship growth. When the congregation was started–before we settled in at our current address–it was a freelance church; so our time out of the building meant a return to the early days.

When heating pipe leaks under the sanctuary required New Horizon Christian Church, Akron, Ohio, to move its worship services to the basement-level fellowship hall for six months, Pastor Jim Bane turned it into a positive. "We can make it like a family room, provide coffee, put the communion table in the middle, and have creative times of worship," he told them. He used the summer months to preach a series on Old Testament stories and titled the series, "Stories from the Basement." People responded well. The net effect of the experience was to enrich people's experience, liberate them from routine, and remind them of the true heart of worship.

Facilitate Healing

Congregational leaders must balance their attention to the larger interests of the church with the personal needs of those the crisis impacted. Every organizational leader, whether secular or sectarian, balances these polarities. Congregational leaders feel this need in an amplified way, since pastoral care lies at the heart of their calling. Whether they lead a large church or a small church, whether they have a support team of skilled, caring people or bear primary responsibility for pastoral care, whether their spiritual gifts and interests predispose them to empathetic care or not, they must steward the needs of those they shepherd.

Shepherding interests may well extend beyond the membership of the congregation. Several of the pastors I interviewed spoke of the ways their crisis care extended into the community. They saw themselves as parish ministers. Their leadership responses to crisis included strategic concern for anyone impacted by the crisis, whether member or not. Wedgwood Baptist Church, for instance, extended its care for the traumatized by working closely with public schools in the community and with Southwestern Baptist Theological Seminary, which lost one former and two current students in the tragedy.

Community disasters, by definition, put this into play. After Hurricane Katrina, our efforts at First Baptist Shreveport were entirely related to nonmembers who showed up in Shreveport from southern Louisiana. Crosspointe Church in Novi, Michigan, dealt with a financial crisis in the region that touched everyone's life in the community around the church. Their ministries of service were aimed intentionally at nonmembers as well as members.

Crisis Care from a Leadership Perspective

As I mentioned in chapter 3, crisis care from a leadership perspective brings strategic awareness to its caring concern. This strategic awareness connects crisis care to crisis leadership. The leadership mind-set takes the caring response beyond palliative response. Leaders aren't just in the trenches reacting to the needs of people with mercy and help. They're also stepping back to reflect on the scale of the needs (how many people have been affected and to what degree?), the short-term and long-term nature of people's needs, the available resources for addressing those needs, and the strategies that should be put into play accordingly.

Crisis care from a leadership perspective also empowers rather than creates dependency relationships. It is asset-based rather than need-based. It activates others in the caring process. Ross Parsley at New Life points to the critical role of the church's small groups in its ability to weather its crises.

Not only does this leaderly response protect a caring leader against burnout, but it also stewards and channels the pent-up desire of other caring people to help. Such leaderly response proves much more effective in the long run—especially if the scale of the crisis is such that it traumatized many people. Strategically, leaderly response also facilitates congregational healing and health, in that it empowers people who have been caught off balance by the crisis. One effect of crisis is that people feel out of control.

By giving them meaningful work toward helping others restores their own confidence, they get to experience the resourcefulness that comes from God. This is heartening. They get to see people's resilience and savor the knowledge that they have been God's catalytic agents. This builds hope and gives cause for celebration, all of which help to lift the cloud of crisis from the congregation.

Those with shepherding gifts need to guard against their tendency to create dependency relationships. Our goal is that those with needs will emerge from the crisis stronger than when they fell into it. Our goal is that our church will emerge from the crisis stronger than when it fell into it. Beware of misplaced good intentions and caregiver ego needs. Remain clearly focused as a leader on promoting individual and congregational resilience when developing and implementing a caring response.

Honor the Healing Process

Immediately after First Baptist Shreveport's bus accident, I took steps to refresh my memory about the emotional impact of trauma and best practices related to posttraumatic care. I also welcomed the offer of member and social worker Jamie Scoggin to help coordinate this dimension of congregational response. Our attentiveness to the postaccident needs of people didn't end after the first few days or even weeks. We knew that emotional healing would take time, would vary from person to person, and would require ongoing monitoring.

We were grateful to have people like Reid Doster with whom to consult. Co-coordinator of the Cooperative Baptist Fellowship of Louisiana and an experienced therapist and pastor with training in critical incident response, Reid briefed us on what to expect and the early steps to take with those most closely impacted by the accident. Among the actions he suggested was a postevent debrief with those in the accident, their families, and those in the church involved in postaccident ministry (staff members and volunteers).

We held this debriefing on a Sunday afternoon four weeks after the accident, carefully selecting therapists from the community to facilitate small groups in which those involved could process their experience and talk in a confidential setting about its immediate and ongoing impact. We also used the occasion to provide information for people's ongoing support. After the small group sessions, we gathered the facilitators for a review of their group time, particularly interested to pick up on special needs that might have surfaced.

Beyond this event, we put other initiatives into play to facilitate emotional healing. We referred people to counselors. We established patterns of ongoing pastoral contact with those in the accident and their families. We helped adult volunteers working with youth understand what to watch for related to posttraumatic shock and how to process the experience with them in group and individual contexts. We insisted on counseling for staff members involved in the accident and underwrote their expenses. We marked the calendar for periodic assessments as to how things were going at the three-month, six-month, and one-year marks. The one-year anniversary provided an opportunity to engage the whole congregation in a service of remembrance and hope.

For more on strategies of care related to congregational trauma and grief, I highly recommend congregational consultant Jill Hudson's book, *Congregational Trauma: Caring, Coping, and Learning.*[6] She draws on careful research and her own experiences with congregational crisis to provide resources for congregational healing. In the course of her presentation, one of the churches she features is Northminster Presbyterian Church in Indianapolis, whose pastor and wife were murdered shortly before Christmas in 1996. Leaders of the church (including Hudson herself) developed excellent strategies for taking trauma and grief processes seriously. They formed a congregational care team and established three challenging goals:

1. To provide resources and support for the congregation in managing grief, anger, and other emotions that naturally arise in situations of violent loss
2. In consultation with staff, to anticipate theological issues or matters of faith that may need to be addressed
3. To facilitate and monitor the healing process[7]

They then laid out separate objectives for serving young children, youth adults, the homebound, and staff. Their plan included resources for parents and adult leaders with children and youth. They developed strategies for education, counseling, and ongoing communication. They concentrated particular attention on healing work during the year following the tragedy. Hudson provides several resources related to their work in appendices of her book.

When it comes to emotional recovery after a crisis, shepherd leaders must have a thoughtful longer-term plan in place and stay on top of it. For instance, we know that people who suffer trauma will experience lingering effects, and often they will experience delayed effects. Having a long-term strategy for tending to the need of those who have been traumatized is essential.

Heal from the Inside Out

Beware of the tendency to rush the emotional healing process. Those who reengage life soon after trauma do better than those who remain frozen, but the outward return to normal activity doesn't negate the need to integrate one's traumatic experience into one's personal, interpersonal, and spiritual system. Return to normal activity certainly isn't a substitute for healthy grieving. These processes take time and happen best in a patient, supportive environment. Just as physicians sometimes treat a wound by keeping it open so that it can heal from the inside out, so congregations need to remain open about the lingering emotional effects of crisis, lest wounds heal too quickly on the outside and fester beneath the surface.

We already noted that New Life Church in Colorado Springs discovered in the aftermath of the deadly shooting that unresolved grief remained from Pastor Ted Haggard's scandal-driven resignation. People hadn't been encouraged to talk out their pain. After the shooting, successor pastor Brady Boyd took particular care to see that the church didn't make the same mistake again. He modeled openness in his sermons and other communication with the church. He reinforced the importance of openness with staff and volunteer leaders. He encouraged people to talk and process their pain.

You need not fear that practicing this kind of openness will cause people to cling to their grief. You need not fear that it will slow recovery. Handled appropriately, this openness will actually promote recovery rather than the mere appearance of recovery. In the context of a congregation that remains anchored in the power of God and focused on its God-given vision, the permission to grieve has a restorative effect. It encourages people to name their pain and reclaim their God-given resilience.

Years ago, a wise pastor explained the resilience factor to me in response to fears I had about getting stuck in my own grief at the time. As an illustration, he pointed to what happens when children fall and scrape their knee. They break into tears and run to their parent. After a little tender loving care and a Band-Aid, they bounce right back and start playing again. This spirit of resilience comes into play even when the scrapes and bruises of childhood give way to serious trauma in those young and old.

Become Wounded Healers

One of the wonderful antidotes to woundedness is compassionate service. Our experiences of suffering can make us more empathetic toward others who suffer and inspire us to encourage and support them. This gives some value to our experience of misfortune, transforming it in redemptive ways.

Author, professor, and priest Henri Nouwen popularized this idea in his book, *The Wounded Healer.*[8] He described how we "can make [our] own wounds available as a source of healing."[9] I was struck over the course of my research by the way crisis-tested pastors and their congregations used their experiences to serve other traumatized congregations.

In the aftermath of Hurricane Charley, CUCC of Punta Gorda received gifts from other congregations, among them a $200 gift from a small, elderly congregation in Hawaii who wrote to say they felt a special kinship, having experienced Hurricane Iniki in 1992. CUCC paid this kindness forward with the $20,000 remaining after its repairs and remodeling. They gave it all away–to a church in Port Charlotte, Florida, a United Church of Christ–related Community Mission in Biloxi, Mississippi, and area families with special needs. As another expression of wounded healing, fifteen months after Hurricane Charley, Pastor Bill Klossner traveled to New Orleans to encourage pastors there who were dealing with the aftereffects of Hurricane Katrina.

Communicate Continuously

Communication plays an essential role in ongoing recovery. People in and beyond the church have an interest in continuing developments. Complications arise that have to be explained and processed. Decisions have to be made that require congregational buy-in. The mind-set and mood of the church has to be nurtured.

Those most closely involved in the task of recovery have to guard against the tendency to become isolated from those beyond the crisis management team. They can become so task focused that they forget the relational nature of their work. This may be the number one shortcoming that crisis leaders acknowledged over the course of my research. I know from years of personal experience how easy it is to let this side of leadership slip.

When communication slips, the congregation gets restless, trust levels suffer, morale declines, unnecessary conflict surfaces, and complications grow. When leaders handle the communication challenge well, congregations stay calm, trust levels grow, morale improves, conflicts ease, and complications get resolved. Effective communication reflects the deep conviction that "we're in this together!" It keeps the congregation working collaboratively in the direction of full recovery.

Provide Communication Updates

To boost your communication, appoint a designated communication coordinator to your crisis management team. They then take it upon themselves to develop a communication plan and keep it going. They make sure the crisis management team includes ongoing communication in its deliberations. They work with others to disseminate information. They manage two-way interaction between congregation and task team.

Depending on the size of your church and the availability of leadership, you may not have someone else to take this role. You may be the closest thing to a communication specialist that your congregation has. If that's the case, then responsibility rests with you to provide regular updates.

You will naturally think of your congregation first when dealing with the issue of communication, but don't forget to communicate with others too. Keep a list of your primary audiences and make sure you include them in your updates, customizing your message as needed:

- The staff members
- The ongoing leadership team
- The congregation as a whole

- Particular subgroups in the church
- Neighbors to your campus
- The larger community
- Those in the broader community of faith
- Those with whom you do business (insurance providers, accountants, attorneys, suppliers, contractors, etc.)
- The news media

Be Honest

Resist the temptation to communicate good news only. Tell the truth, even when it proves difficult. People handle bad news better than disconnected silence.

In 2007, the Transportation Department of the State of Washington came to Lake Washington Christian Church in Kirkland, Washington, saying they wanted the church's property for freeway expansion. The church decided to resist initially, contacting attorneys and launching a legal process that lasted two years. Eventually, resistance shifted into negotiating the terms of a sale, which was finalized in 2009. The church moved into temporary quarters, then bought an existing church building. Throughout the process, Pastor Kerry Grogan and other crisis leaders kept the congregation informed. This included breaking bad news as it became clear that they wouldn't be able to stay at their original location. Effective communication made it possible for the church to wrestle together with questions of identity, vision, and mission and to coalesce around an answer to the question, "Where will we go?"

Manage Expectations

Effective communication makes it easier to manage expectations. Unrealistic hopes and false assumptions can lead people to underestimate the time, money, or emotional energy that recovery will require. When we keep current with our communication, we give people a better fix on where things stand and what lies ahead.

We live in a thirty-minute sitcom culture that looks for quick, easy solutions to every difficulty. Congregational crises don't lend themselves to this approach. Emotional recovery takes time. Personnel search processes can't be predicted. Construction delays are the rule rather than the exception. Legal matters put us in a pipeline filled with uncertainty. Crises, in other words, create a period of suspended animation, and people need regular injections of realism to keep this in perspective.

The leadership team at University Baptist of Waco decided to wait one year after Kyle Lake's death to hire a new community pastor. It waited two years before calling a new teaching pastor. Its communication with the congregation about a more patient, deliberative approach was an essential aspect of its managing the crisis recovery process.

Managing expectations proves a lot easier if it goes hand in hand with a concerted effort to put the congregation back on track. The congregation needs to understand the current issues, what's being done to deal with them, what the prospects are for their resolution, and what–if anything–they can do to help. University Baptist's ability to wait for a new teaching pastor was aided by their having a clearly articulated plan that was unfolding appropriately.

In all circumstances members can be asked to pray, turning their concern and goodwill toward intercession. Praying will undoubtedly be the most important contribution anyone makes toward congregational renewal.

Mark Progress

By all means, make sure you call attention to good news and reinforce the things people are doing to promote recovery. Catch people in the act of doing the right things and affirm their efforts. Celebrate milestones along the way. Sandy Run Baptist Church made a major production of their groundbreaking ceremony when it came time to replace their burned-out sanctuary by involving everyone in attendance in the actual groundbreaking.

Remember holidays and anniversary dates as particularly meaningful times in the healing process. Grief grows stronger at these times. We remember and miss the people, places, and things we've lost. The first anniversary is particularly poignant. Effective leaders understand the power of creative rituals to mark these occasions. They call attention to the moment from the pulpit. They target their writing toward those who grieve. They provide a gathering place and time to comfort people in their loss and honor their memories. One year after a gunman took the lives of two sisters at New Life Church in Colorado Springs, people gathered at a special memorial in an area of the parking lot near where the shootings had occurred. Two benches and two trees marked their lives, and the crowd rallied together in tears and praise to affirm their faith in God.

The Road to Recovery

Crisis leadership is a long-distance run, not a sprint. Though every congregational crisis has its own unique characteristics and varies in terms of damage, duration, and disruption, all congregational crises pose complex challenges for those who lead. Those who lead faithfully, however long it takes, gain the pleasure of shepherding their congregations through the difficulties toward a new lease on life.

Reflection Questions

Reflect personally on the following questions. If you are using this book with a study group, share your perspectives with each other. If you aren't currently experiencing a congregational crisis, think of a crisis your congregation has experienced or might experience and project yourself into that situation when reflecting on the questions.

- How would you express the goal of your congregation's response to crisis? Toward what end are you aiming?
- What are your key objectives? What clearly defined, decisive, attainable outcomes will you pursue to attain your goal?
- What are your principal caring concerns at this stage? How can they be addressed in keeping with the leadership orientation toward caring in chapter 3?

Congregations in Focus

New Life Church, Colorado Springs, Colorado

One major crisis can put a congregation out of commission. What are the chances that a church can survive two major crises in a little over a year? New Life Church, a nondenominational charismatic megachurch in Colorado Springs, Colorado, stands as testimony to the possibility. Not only has it survived, but it has found ways to thrive again after multiple traumas.

Under the leadership of its founding pastor, Ted Haggard, New Life Church grew to an estimated fourteen thousand members and gained worldwide attention for its worship and prayer ministries and its cultural and political engagement. Haggard became a prominent public figure, stepping into the role of president of the National Association of Evangelicals in 2003.

Scandal, not success, became the cause of worldwide attention on November 2, 2006. Haggard yielded his position as pastor after news broke that he had paid a male escort for sex for three years and used illegal drugs. Under the glare of the media spotlight, the church experienced the shock of its unwelcome circumstances and took steps to move forward and heal. A nine-person pastoral selection committee was named. The board of overseers selected New Life's music ministry pastor Ross Parsley as interim senior pastor.

During the first couple of months after the scandal broke, New Life lost about 20 percent of its members. Participation eventually stabilized. Parsley points to several factors that contributed to New Life's ability to weather the storm:

- A healthy network of small groups
- A strong worship dynamic

- A vibrant prayer ministry
- A stable leadership team
- A decentralized ministry culture

It also helped that Parsley brought sixteen years of congregational leadership and relationship into his role as interim pastor.

Symbolic of the congregation's commitment to be Christ centered rather than human leader centered, it refused to let the news of November 2 keep it from continuing its practice of dedicating babies on the first Sunday of every month. On Sunday, November 5, Parsley invited parents to bring their babies forward, and the church committed each child to Jesus. This was followed by twenty minutes of full-throated worship of God.

The church's recovery crossed an important threshold on August 27, 2007, with the election of Brady Boyd to replace Ted Haggard as senior pastor. Then barely one hundred days into Boyd's ministry, crisis struck again. On Sunday, December 9, 2007, twenty-four-year-old Matthew Murray appeared on campus after morning worship and began shooting, injuring four people and killing two before being shot by church security volunteer Jeanne Assam and then taking his own life.

How did New Life manage to absorb two staggering blows in quick succession and stay on its feet? Not surprisingly, congregational leaders focus on God as the ultimate source of their resiliency and worship, prayer, and strength of fellowship as the key assets God used to sustain them.

On the Wednesday night following the shooting, a sea tide of New Lifers rolled into "The Living Room," the church's worship center. In the company of a large contingent of public officials and first responders they worshiped God and announced their refusal to let crisis derail them. Pastor Boyd would later say,

> We decided that night that we were going to bond together, that we were going to worship like we had never worshiped, that we were going to pray like we had never prayed. The healing didn't happen right away, but it started that night.

Leaders didn't leave the healing to chance. They made arrangements with one hundred professional counselors to serve the staff and church members. They leveraged the strength of their small group system to help deal with the trauma and sustain fellowship. Boyd says, "People didn't scatter because the sense of community was woven into the fabric of our life together."

The second crisis exposed wounds from the first crisis that hadn't healed. The congregation resisted the temptation to gloss over the impact of their crises out of embarrassment or a false notion of faith. Members were encouraged to take off their masks and talk honestly with each other about their pain, anger, fear, and grief. Pastor Boyd modeled this openness in his preaching, his pastoral care, his blogging, and his dealings with the omnipresent media.

He also asserted a biblical vision big enough to embrace suffering:

> We don't pursue suffering, but we know it's not *if,* but *when* suffering will come. As Jesus stated in John 16:33, "In this world you will have tribulation, but be of good cheer! I have overcome the world." Our crises have given me fresh license to talk about this.

The church created a memorial at the spot on the parking lot where teenage sisters Rachel and Stephanie Works were killed and their father wounded. On the first anniversary of the shooting, and on a smaller scale the following year, people gathered at the memorial for a candlelight vigil involving testimony, song, and prayer. The memorial continues to be a place where people can place flowers or sit for prayer and reflection on one of two benches under the shade of two spruce trees that were planted there.

Through both crises, the congregation's clearly established patterns of governance provided welcome clarity when needed most. In keeping with church bylaws, the board of elders stepped into the breach when the Haggard scandal broke, dealing directly with Haggard, communicating with the church, setting up processes for the interim and the search for a new senior pastor, and monitoring the congregation's ongoing developments. The board of overseers, a group of five outside pastors, did yeoman service too, providing spiritual guidance and support to congregational leaders in the aftermath of both crises. The church staff and other ministry leaders did their part to keep the church focused on ministry and mission.

The ripple effects of crisis didn't suddenly stop at some magic moment on the calendar. As recently as January 2009, the church found itself in the media eye again when it confirmed that in 2006, the board of elders had reached a six-figure settlement with a young male in the church who had accused Haggard of an inappropriate, ongoing relationship. The revelation reopened old wounds. Attendance and giving, which had dropped in the aftermath of the Haggard scandal, dropped once again.

As an essential element in restoring trust, Pastor Boyd and the rest of the leadership team elected to talk openly about what had happened. They also elected to keep the congregation focused on its mission and vision. It took months for tail winds to pick up again. In one of his October 2009 blogs, Boyd wrote to his congregation about a return of momentum in June of that year, as the church looked ahead rather than dwelling on the past. Boyd wrote,

> This summer, we did just that. We became convinced that God had not removed his lamp stand from New Life and we should get busy with our assignment. We began to dream about taking care of widows, orphans, and the poor. We began to dream about planting life giving churches around the world. We began to serve the needs of our city, and we made a choice to pray with fervor and passion. We are not moving real fast right now, but we are moving forward.[1]

New Life Church continues to learn and grow in the aftermath of its experiences. Its resilience serves as notice that churches can weather multiple storms and keep going, in the strength of God.

6

Finding a New Normal

Resolving Crisis

By its very nature, crisis disrupts the *normal* life of the church and becomes an all-consuming focus of attention. Furthermore, it creates short-term and long-term ripple effects that must be managed. That being said, a crisis doesn't last forever. Congregations, like individuals, have a built-in impulse toward the restoration of order. Eventually, things settle down again and congregational life goes on. The congregation finds its way to *a new normal.*

This doesn't mean that a congregation will automatically resolve its crisis in healthy ways. Things can end up better or worse than before, but they will never be the same. Crisis leadership will have a significant impact on how desirable the outcomes will be.

As already established, crisis leadership plays an essential role at the *outset of crisis* (chapter 4) and during the longer process of *crisis recovery* (chapter 5). Let's now consider the role of leadership in the *resolution of crisis*. What's the end game? How do leaders facilitate a healthy conclusion to crisis?

Acknowledging the Importance of Closure

To begin with, congregational leaders facilitate a healthy conclusion to crisis by acknowledging the importance of closure. Congregational crises, when handled well, are like the age-old description of the month of March: they come in like a lion and go out like a lamb. Their fierceness dissipates and congregational health prevails. One of the implications of this is that whereas it's *hard* to miss the onset of crisis, it's *easy* to miss its resolution.

Why does this matter? Consider these reasons:

1. *People have a psychological need for closure.* Closure helps them put a period at the end of a disruptive chapter of the congregation's story so as to take measure of what happened and fully give themselves to the next chapter.
2. *Loose ends always appear as a crisis reaches resolution.* Seeing crisis resolution within reach motivates a congregation to deal with those loose ends.
3. *The resolution of crisis presents a golden opportunity for congregational development.* The end of a crisis provides a notable occasion for thanking God, affirming congregational strengths, and harvesting insight for the future. You can't take full advantage of these opportunities if you allow the moment to pass without notice.

Leaders who appreciate the value of closure are more likely to stay on top of the crisis recovery process and finish it well. This has an empowering effect on the congregations they serve.

Knowing When to Say "When"

Having affirmed the value of closure, one question naturally follows: When is it time to say "When"? How do you know the crisis either has ended or has neared an end?

One way to answer this is to say that the crisis ends when the issues created by your crisis have been resolved—that is, when your church's crisis-resolution objectives have been reached (see chapter 5). If you took time at the outset of your recovery process to establish specific, decisive, attainable objectives then you have clear criteria for marking the finish line.

This isn't to suggest that you can reduce crisis recovery to a simple checklist. Some aspects of recovery are qualitative rather than quantitative, and you will want to consider this when clarifying your objectives in the first place. You will have objectives that can't be measured in terms of attendance, contributions, or project completion. They have to be measured in terms of mood and mind-set. You will have to look for anecdotal evidence that the cloud of crisis has lifted. Prayerful intuition will come into play.

You also have to allow for the possibility that you will revise the objectives along the way to create a more realistic finish line. Consider, for instance, First Baptist Shreveport's post-bus-accident recovery.

First Baptist's recovery took shape around objectives related to seven issues:

1. *Medical issues.* We wanted critical medical issues resolved and survivors reengaged in their daily lives.
2. *Insurance issues.* We wanted insurance obligations sorted out and settled in a way that was fair to all concerned.

3. *Legal issues.* We wanted legal liability issues sorted out and settled in a way that was fair to all concerned.
4. *Operational issues.* We wanted accident-affected staff back at work and engaged in routine activity, the church reengaged in normal activity, and administrative disruptions resolved.
5. *Personal care issues.* We wanted the grief and emotional trauma of accident victims, their families, and the congregation to subside; immediate counseling concerns to be identified and addressed; and a plan put in place for dealing with the long-term effects of posttraumatic stress. We also wanted accident victims and their families to feel that the church had been appropriately attentive to their medical, insurance, legal, and personal concerns.
6. *Media issues.* We wanted to be known more for our positive, faith-filled response to the crisis than for the crisis itself. We also wanted to stay in front of the news related to ongoing developments by interacting with the media in a timely, responsive way.
7. *Missional issues.* We wanted the congregation to experience a boost of confidence, greater unity in its diversity, and a heightened sense of missional purpose as a result of its response to the crisis.

We resolved some of these issues more readily than others. Those who survived the accident got better. Injured staff got back to work, and the programmatic life of the church got back on track. Media attention subsided after providing countless opportunities for us to point to the goodness of God and put our faith and resiliency on display. The church experienced a boost of confidence and esprit de corps, just as we had hoped.

Other aspects of our crisis resisted resolution. Some of the grief ran deep and would continue for some time to come. Some of the trauma, by its very nature, was likely to have an ongoing effect. Furthermore, questions of liability brought into play the insurance companies and attorneys of the bus manufacturer, the tire manufacturer, the church, and those involved in the accident. This, in turn, complicated our ability to respond in a timely and gracious manner to the concerns of some of the affected families, especially as it had to do with responsibility for medical expenses. We had to adjust our objectives out of the realization that we would continue to deal with insurance and legal issues after the central crisis had concluded.

For the most part, the issues that remained unresolved after three months eventually slipped from center stage to side stage. They were managed behind the scenes, at a leadership, administrative, and pastoral level and no longer dominated the attention of the whole congregation or disrupted its ongoing life. By the time First Baptist held a service of remembrance and hope on the first anniversary of the bus accident, its crash-related crisis had come to an end.

How long a congregation's crisis lasts will vary widely, though the intensity of a crisis generally only lasts one to three months, after which it takes on a different character. The only crises that remain intense for longer periods of time are those involving continued uncertainty and waves of new distress.

It's not realistic to think that every last particle has to be resolved before you can declare the crisis at an end. After an accident, for instance, people may deal with chronic health issues, as was the case with more than one of the seven survivors of the Wedgwood Baptist shooting. Particular individuals may still be working their way through grief or posttraumatic shock, as is almost always the case with those most profoundly impacted by a crisis-related loss.

The family and close friends of University Baptist of Waco pastor Kyle Lake experienced depths of grief after his sudden death that lingered beyond the immobilizing grief of congregational crisis. A time came when this became a matter of friendship and pastoral care rather than crisis care, and the grief of individuals was no longer front page news. Congregation-wide grief resolves itself more quickly than the grief of those most closely connected to the crisis.

Legal issues may not be fully resolved before a crisis is resolved. First Baptist Shreveport isn't in crisis mode any more, even though legal issues remain. Church leaders are still dealing with these issues behind the scenes. The church will continue to receive occasional reports about developments in this regard, but the church has moved on.

If you have been intimately involved in a crisis as a congregational leader, you would do well to evaluate your own mental and emotional state as crisis-related issues near resolution. What is your current level of disorientation or anxiety or grief or posttraumatic shock? If you're still traumatized, it will affect those around you. Your condition will infect the congregation as a whole.

This was one of the concerns of John Henson, associate pastor of First Baptist Shreveport, whose daughter died as a result of injuries suffered in the bus accident. He had to process his grief in a way different from the congregation. He had to manage his emotions as he experienced the church at a different level of readiness to move beyond grief or to celebrate God's providence as it related to accident survivors. The counterpart was also true. The congregation had to figure out a way to love the Hensons and honor their grief without getting stuck in its own sadness.

Signs of Crisis Resolution

Any number of things can signal that your congregation is moving beyond crisis mode.

Some of these are quantifiable:

- Crisis recovery action items get taken care of
- Attendance stabilizes or even improves

- A trend of new guests and members develops
- Damaged buildings get repaired or replaced
- The congregation's financials look solid again

New Life Church of Colorado Springs lost members after each of their crises, but then attendance stabilized and new people began to show up. Anxiety over participation trends subsided.

Sandy Run Baptist's and New Horizon Christian's attendance held up during their dislocations because of fire and leaking pipes, respectively. They saw this as confirmation that they had weathered the crisis well. It helped them put the crisis behind them. The completion and dedication of their new space became a defining moment, signaling that their crises had come to an end.

Holmeswood Baptist Church of Kansas City had a successful steward-ship experience to point to as evidence that their financial crisis had passed. On a single Sunday, their projected budget deficit turned into a pledged budget surplus. Crosspointe Meadows in Novi, Michigan, put its financial crisis to bed not by some miraculous turnaround in giving but by creating ministries to serve people in financial distress, postponing its plans to build, and adjusting ministry plans to live within its means. The ability to live within its means while still carrying on creative ministry became a notable sign to the congregation that it was weathering the storm.

Qualitative Developments. Qualitative developments can also signal crisis resolution. You can create congregational surveys to measure these developments, but most congregations lean on anecdotal evidence and prayerful intuition to gauge that

- the congregation's losses have been accepted (this has to do with grief resolution);
- the congregation can look back at its crisis circumstances without feel-ing traumatized;
- changes growing out of the crisis have been embraced;
- trust has been restored;
- missional energy has returned;
- a spirit of joy, laughter, and celebration has been infused again into the life of the church.

In a pastoral blog on April 14, 2009, New Life pastor Brady Boyd exemplified this kind of intuitive awareness when he wrote,

> Sunday, I sensed a renewed energy in the people of New Life and a new sense of forward momentum. I think this happened because so many people committed themselves to something that required strength from heaven and the use of their unique spiritual gifts.

When we surrender ourselves to the call and purposes of God, heaven responds with power and strength that literally propels us forward, like a ship charging across the waves.[1]

Clearly, Pastor Boyd was picking up on tangible evidence and other intangibles to draw his conclusion. Together, these developments pointed to renewed congregational enthusiasm. They gave evidence of a congregation that had emerged from crisis.

Pivotal Events. Congregational leaders frequently point to pivotal events as releasing their congregation toward postcrisis life. For University Baptist of Waco, the hiring of Josh Carney as teaching pastor, two years after Kyle Lake's death, was that pivotal event. It reflected the congregation's sense that it was OK to move on.

For Wedgwood Baptist of Fort Worth, the March 20, 2002, dedication of a memorial to its seven shooting victims proved pivotal. During an emotional, two-hour service, those in attendance honored those who had died, celebrated life, and declared their confidence in God.

New Horizon's recovery from leaking pipes came in stages, culminating in two pivotal events. First, the congregation returned to the sanctuary and rededicated the space for worship during Advent 2008. Second, since part of the fundraising for sanctuary renovation also included funding for a new staff person for community ministries, the arrival of a person into that role in January 2010 solidified the sense that the congregation had moved on.

First Baptist, Norman, Oklahoma, was shaken by the short tenures—two years each—of two pastors in a row after the previous two pastors had served a combined total of seventy-five years. I was the first of those short-tenured pastors. Current pastor Wade Smith points to his second anniversary as a pivotal event for the congregation. When members realized Wade had settled in for the long haul, they were able to let go of their anxiety about losing another pastor and let him and his family into their lives at a whole new level. The mood of the congregation brightened, and the ministries of the church gained fresh momentum.

For one pastor, who preferred not to be named, the pivotal moment after an embezzlement crisis came during a pastoral visit in the home of an eighty-five-year-old widow, who also happened to be a bellwether of the church. He knew it was time to move forward when this wise, elderly member said, "Pastor, we've had enough of it. I don't want you to keep talking about it. You don't need to hear any more of my whining. We need to turn toward being faithful!"

The notable signs and moments that the crisis is ending will vary from church to church and from crisis to crisis. In cases of conflict or scandal, you will experience evidence of grace, forgiveness, love, and renewed trust. After the loss of a leader, you will experience the resolution of grief, the arrival of a new leader, or the sense that the newer leader is being embraced for who she or he is. The completion of a construction project may well signal the end of a crisis related to damaged property, though other factors will have an impact on this too. Consider the case of Sandy Run Baptist. Many of the church's members had multigenerational ties to the sanctuary that went up in flames. The crisis ended for them not when Sandy Run dedicated the new facility but when their resolution of grief allowed them to accept what they had lost and embrace what had taken its place.

Let me complicate this conversation a bit by noting that crisis resolution for congregations differs from crisis resolution in corporations in at least one very specific way: congregational crisis often lingers longer because of the level at which the entire membership participates in the crisis and its resolution. Congregational crises don't just pose technical problems that have to be fixed, they also pose psychosocial problems that have to be resolved.

I don't think this is actually unique to congregational life. Organizations of any kind have these issues going on, and the best organizations pay attention to these issues in the way they manage the crisis resolution process, such as providing counselors for employees, offering individual and group debriefs and therapy, evaluating employee morale, and so on. Very little of the literature in the field of business, however, builds this into the plan or includes this factor in its calculation of time for crisis resolution.

If I were to rely on technical definitions and parameters for determining the resolution of a crisis, I would locate resolution earlier in time than did the pastors with whom I spoke. Technically speaking, a crisis won't last more than six to nine weeks. What accounts for the fact that pastors consistently saw their crises as lasting anywhere from several months to multiple years?

Several explanations suggest themselves. For one thing, congregations have an inherently relational character about them. We are the "body of Christ," the "family of God." Essential to our purpose is loving God and loving one another. Processing people's pain isn't an adjunct to our central business, it's part of our core business.

So while wise congregational leaders get their congregations back on track as quickly as possible with the core activity of the congregation, they continue to pay considerable attention to the congregation's emotional temperature. They don't consider the crisis truly resolved until the congregation shares a prevailing sense that they have processed their pain, resolved their grief, regained their confidence, embraced their new trajectory, and given themselves with enthusiasm to a renewed vision of their future under God.

That's what Brady Boyd kept looking for and finally saw, which prompted him to write in his pastor's blog that New Life Church had turned a corner. The spirit of the congregation had returned.

Consider what this means from a biblical-faith perspective. We talk about "the spirit of the congregation," and we mean this literally. The Greek and Hebrew words for "spirit" can also be translated as "breath" or "wind." God's Spirit breathes life into us and moves in us and among us like the wind. The apostle Paul once declared that "in [God] we live and breathe and have our being" (Acts 17:28), affirming that every breath we take is, in one sense, God's Spirit breathing into and out of us. As soon as God stops breathing into and out of us, we cease to live.

The Bible portrays corporate expressions of this as well. Our existence as the people of God comes when God's Spirit is poured out on us (Joel 2:28–29). When God's Spirit is removed, everything falls apart (1 Samuel 4:21).

So we join a long history of the people of God when we consider this dimension of a congregation's life and look for signs that God's Spirit has breathed fresh life into us. Crises take the wind out of us; we count on God to work through the healing processes of the congregation to give our breath back to us.

For good reason, we call this intrinsically spiritual and therefore intangible quality of our life together *enthusiasm*, which literally means "indwelt by God." Congregational leaders look for signs that enthusiasm has returned after the gut punch of crisis.

Leaders look for tangible evidence of this intangible reality. For Wedgwood Baptist, one of the signs that its crisis had passed was that people could talk about what had happened without feeling traumatized. For First Baptist Shreveport, one of the signs was that laughter had returned. University Baptist of Waco's leaders saw evidence of grief resolution in the fact that they could make ministry decisions without constantly referring back to Kyle Lake as a reference point. This freedom to embrace a fresh future has now reached the point where it has become healthy, as current pastor Josh Carney puts it, to "reinsert Kyle Lake's voice" into the congregation. When I spoke with Josh, the church was using one of Kyle's benedictions regularly.

What to Do as a Crisis Comes to an End

When consensus develops among your congregational leaders that your congregation has reached the point of crisis resolution, consider taking specific steps to reinforce the return of positive momentum. Before turning away from the crisis entirely, make sure your congregation finishes the journey of crisis recovery well.

Wrap Up Loose Ends

Do some elements of your crisis recovery plan still need tending? The crisis management team will want to use this moment to review its action items for unfinished business. Based on the objectives you laid out, it can also prove helpful to ask yourselves if any action steps need to be taken that hadn't been considered before. Are there bills to pay, finishing touches to add, affected families to visit, or leaders to debrief and formally release from special assignments? Are there promises made that haven't been fulfilled yet?

Your loose ends will be unique to your situation. During the second Sunday of Advent, 2008, New Horizon Christian Church in Akron celebrated its return to the sanctuary after repairs and remodeling, but it still had new pews on order. These didn't get delivered and installed until the following spring.

Document Everything Significant That Happened

Hopefully, you have (and/or someone else has) accumulated a file with a record of deliberations, decisions, and developments related to the crisis and the recovery process. Now is the time to make sure you have collected all relevant information. You and the rest of the crisis management team can decide what information is relevant for you.

Even under normal circumstances, the discipline of record keeping eludes the leadership groups of many congregations. The challenge escalates in times of crisis. Who has time to worry about record keeping when other things demand urgent attention? It may seem like an unaffordable luxury to take time for documentation, but you'll be glad you did in the long run. This material has importance not only for historical preservation purposes but also for project completion, postcrisis learning, and future planning.

During World War II, the U.S. Navy tasked Harvard University historian and naval reserve officer Samuel Eliot Morison to chronicle the war at sea. He, in turn, recruited a team of fellow researchers. By the end of the war, their collective effort produced a fifteen-volume work from which naval students, strategists, and tacticians draw lessons to this day.[2]

We'll talk more in the next chapter about learning from your crisis experience. For now, make sure you have captured and preserved the essential record of your experience. While the crisis is still relatively fresh, take time—individually and as a crisis management team—to itemize significant developments and fill in blanks of information that may not have been preserved.

Publicly Mark the End of the Crisis (But Don't Be Premature)

As was stated earlier, crises come in like a lion and go out like a lamb. This means that they can end simply by fading from congregational awareness. That's what happens when problems get solved; the cloud of concern lifts, and a congregation's focus turns back in a positive, forward-looking direction. Congregational resilience is a good thing.

Still, spiritual, administrative, and motivational reasons call us to mark the end of the crisis in a formal, public way. First and foremost, we don't want the moment to pass without giving thanks to God. We counted on God's providence in the midst of our crisis, and God came through. The end of a crisis offers an occasion for calling attention to the goodness of God and expressing out loud what our grateful hearts feel. When Sandy Run Baptist Church dedicated its new sanctuary in March 2010, this is exactly what happened.

Saying thanks may or may not involve an atmosphere of giddy cel-ebration. At First Baptist Shreveport, Wedgwood Baptist of Fort Worth, and New Life Church of Colorado Springs, respect for those who had lost loved ones tempered the approach to thanksgiving. At the dedication of a memorial to its seven shooting victims on March 30, 2002, Wedgwood Baptist attendees heard from family members of some of the victims, shed tears, and acknowledged the trauma of the event. Still, Pastor Al Meredith called the service a celebration of life.

From an administrative standpoint, people who have taken on special assignments or made interim adjustments because of the crisis need a clear signal that they can move out of crisis mode. They also need clear guidance about what the new normal means for them, given that organizational pat-terns may have changed permanently as a result of the crisis. During my time as a board member of Central Baptist Theological Seminary (CBTS) in the metropolitan area of Kansas City, a budget crisis led the board to declare a state of financial exigency, a necessary precursor to making administrative, personnel, and campus changes to restabilize the institution. Tenured faculty members graciously accepted the temporary loss of job security that came with the declaration. Some lost their jobs to downsiz-ing. Over the ensuing months, CBTS took decisive steps to get back on track, finding new and creative ways to fulfill its mission while developing and living within its means. Criteria had been established for determining when the seminary could exit the state of financial exigency, and when these criteria had been satisfied, the board took formal action to declare it at an end. The faculty representative to the board played an important role in the deliberations that preceded formal action, expressing on behalf of the faculty and other employees their need for clear and formal notice that the period of suspended animation had ended.

Spiritual and administrative reasons call us to mark the end of a crisis publicly. Motivational reasons echo the same call. The end of a crisis offers a golden opportunity to affirm the resilience of your people and their dedica-tion to the mission, vision, and values that you share. You can recap what the congregation has gone through and highlight specific ways they have demonstrated congregational wellness. You can point to specific ways the congregation's response to crisis has strengthened it and blessed others. You can buoy everyone's confidence in the faithfulness of God. You can encourage their ongoing faithfulness as the congregation moves ahead.

That's what New Life of Colorado Springs pastor Brady Boyd was doing with his blog entry on October 12, 2009, when seeing signs of renewed momentum ("Big Mo"), he wrote,

> New Life lost "Big Mo" after two very dark days that happened 13 months apart in 2006 and 2007. The results of those two cataclys-mic events were devastating on many fronts. Trust was broken, our innocence was lost, and our world seemed to be crashing in

around us. The Holy Spirit never left us, and God's love was very real to us; but "Big Mo" was nowhere to be found.

Then he suddenly reappeared at New Life in June of this year like a Christmas miracle . . . You see, "Big Mo" loves the windshield and not the rearview mirror. He hangs out with people who are looking ahead and not dwelling in the past. This summer, we did just that.[3]

Whether in worship and other church gatherings, or through Web site, e-mail, newsletter, or at staff and other leadership meetings, let people know that the crisis has passed. Help your people put a punctuation mark at the end of the experience. Clearly mark the occasion for closing the crisis chapter of your congregation's story and moving on to the new and hope-filled chapter that comes next.

The Residue of Crisis

Depending on the nature of your congregation's crisis, its end may not be the last you see of it. Moments may come down the road when you find yourself dealing with its long-term effects.

As I wrote the first draft of this chapter, momentous news came that Al Qaeda head and 9/11 mastermind Osama bin Laden had been killed by a U.S. special ops team. Crowds gathered in front of the White House to celebrate. As word filtered around the stadium at a nationally televised baseball game in Philadelphia between the New York Mets and the Philadelphia Phillies, the crowd began chanting "U-S-A! U-S-A!" It will be one of those moments people recall well enough to say exactly where they were when they got the news. It marks another milestone in the nation's healing, nine and a half years after the horrific events of 9/11.

Crises resolve themselves in stages. Life goes on. We find a new normal. But this doesn't mean that we forget what happened or that we get beyond any emotional sensitivity related to the crisis. Things can happen that stir up old feelings. Things can happen that reinforce our appreciation for how life has gone on. We can experience things that cause us to see just how deeply and permanently we have been marked by the crisis. As Pastor Al Meredith puts it, "We haven't gotten over it, but we have gotten through it."

In the years ahead, parents of youth at First Baptist Shreveport will have the accident of 2009 in the back of their minds when their kids get on a bus for an out-of-town trip. To this day, twelve years after a gunman shattered the peace of its congregation, some Wedgwood members express heightened anxiety when odd-looking, odd-acting strangers show up for worship.

Even when the sensitivities subside, our memories of the crisis linger. In fact, that's how it should be. The goal of emotional healing from crisis isn't forgetting, after all. The goal of emotional healing is what professor and award-winning author Lewis Smedes once termed "redemptive remembering."[4] In keeping with Hebrew tradition, we preserve a clear picture of the defining moments of our lives, while experiencing release from the trauma. God invites us to see the past through the lens of God's deliverance rather than through the lens of our suffering. As Psalm 103 puts it,

> Bless the Lord, O my soul,
> and do not forget all his benefits—
> who forgives all your iniquity,
> who heals all your diseases,
> who redeems your life from the Pit,
> who crowns you with steadfast love and mercy,
> who satisfies you with good as long as you live
> so that your youth is renewed like the eagle's.
> (Psalm 103:2–5)

Wise congregations memorialize what they've experienced, the people they've loved, and the resilience they've experienced as testimonies to the faithfulness of God. University Baptist of Waco has incorporated memories of Kyle Lake into its life, its worship, and its building. New Life has created a memorial in the parking lot near where the two sisters were shot and killed. Wise congregations memorialize, but not to cling to the past. They memorialize to give themselves a reference point that reinforces their vision and values. They memorialize to inspire forward momentum.

Crises don't last forever. A new normal comes. In the grace of God, that new normal can be very good indeed. Let's turn our attention now to the kind of leadership that can help that happen. Leaders make sure their congregations learn from trouble.

Reflection Questions

Reflect personally on the following questions. If you are using this book with a study group, share your perspectives with each other. If you aren't currently experiencing a congregational crisis, think of a crisis your congregation has experienced or might experience and project yourself into that situation when reflecting on the questions.

- What quantifiable signs of crisis resolution do you think are most important?
- What are you looking for as qualitative signs that the congregation has reached crisis resolution?
- What do you want to do to wrap things up and mark the end of your congregation's crisis?

Part III

Special Considerations for Congregational Leaders

Congregations in Focus

Crosspointe Meadows Church, Novi, Michigan

When the global economy took a dive in 2008, the Detroit area felt the effects of it in a particularly poignant way. Motor City and its environs still hadn't recovered from the economic aftershocks of the terrorist attacks of September 11, 2001. The auto industry, a cyclical industry under the best of circumstances, teetered under the pressure. Veterans in the marketplace felt concern that General Motors and the Chrysler Corporation might both go bankrupt.

For churches like Crosspointe Meadows Church, an American Baptist congregation in Novi, Michigan, the situation was intensely personal and serious. Eighty percent of Crosspointe's members had auto-related jobs or retirement benefits. At one point at least 20 percent of its members were unemployed. Heads of household were disproportionately affected, having lost their jobs while lower-paid spouses kept theirs.

The situation defied simple solutions. As many as half of those who lost their jobs exhausted their unemployment benefits before finding other work. Most of those who did find other work had to take severe pay cuts. One member, unemployed since 2004, was still looking for employment in 2010.

For Danny Langley, pastor of the church since 1998, the challenge has been to lead the church missionally and compassionately, balancing pragmatism and faith. Leading missionally has meant adapting to unforeseen circumstances without losing focus on the church's God-given purpose. Leading compassionately has meant responding to the special needs and general sense of discouragement that have attended the economic crisis. Balancing pragmatism and faith has meant discerning God's guidance somewhere in the tension between financial realities and ministry possibilities.

Founded as Redford Baptist Church in 1831, the congregation changed its name and moved from Redford Township to Novi in 1998, the year Langley became pastor. It completed the first phase of a five-phase construction plan in May 2008. The first decade of Langley's tenure saw a reversal of the church's aging and decline, with a new core of young adults and a freshly populated nursery. The forty-acre campus master plan called for two-year intervals between construction phases, but as 2010 rolled around, congregational leaders decided to revisit the construction schedule. Despite pressure from some to go ahead and build—"If you build it, they will come" or "You've got to have faith"—the church decided to wait on further economic developments. Danny laughs at the realization that he, normally the voice of courage and faith, has felt it wisest to align himself with the voices of fiscal prudence.

Not surprisingly, capital planning hasn't been the only aspect of the church's ministry to take a hit. A 30 percent downturn in general giving has necessitated some serious belt tightening, with the accompanying requirement that the church rebalance its ministry priorities. Historically affluent, the church had created a staff-dependent vision of ministry; as much as 80 percent of its budget was earmarked for personnel. That percentage now stands at 47–48 percent. Like many churches that build up infrastructures in their heyday and then hold onto them beyond sustainability, Crosspointe had become overstaffed. Now Langley is the only full-time employee, with three part-time employees in the areas of worship, children, and secretarial support.

Necessity has been the mother of invention in another way too. The church has changed its definition of *staff*. Rather than tying the label to salary, it has redefined *staff* as anyone who reports directly to the pastor. This includes volunteer as well as paid leaders in the areas of worship, youth, children, ministry development, leadership development, and administration.

Innovative belt tightening hasn't halted the church's interest in new ministries. In fact, economic circumstances have heightened its sense of connection to the community. It has taken steps to serve those in and beyond its membership who are struggling with debt. An informal survey of church couples forty years old and under revealed an average of $18,000 in credit card debt. This discovery prompted a member of the church to develop a multifaceted financial planning ministry, using Dave Ramsey's thirteen-week video- and discussion-based "Financial Peace University" as a key resource.[1] More than one hundred church and community people had participated in the course as of 2010. The church also introduced a Financial Forum, a once-per-quarter focus on different aspects of money management. The church isn't just thinking about its institutional survival needs;

it has dedicated itself to helping people deal with their own survival needs and develop spiritually healthy financial lives.

In further testimony to Crosspointe Meadows's undaunted commitment to new ministries, the church has taken steps to connect with a large population of Japanese and other Asians who have come to work in the auto industry. In the past, the church would have addressed this interest by hiring a part-time staff person. Now it has decided to explore the possibility of a partnership with a Japanese bivocational pastor in the community.

A regional crisis like the one faced by those in the Detroit area doesn't lend itself to quick fixes. Pastoring people as they cope with long-term unemployment and drastically altered financial prospects has stretched Langley's capacity to care. While shepherding members and leading the church to reinvent itself, he has had to pay attention to the cumulative toll such stress has taken on him and his family. He has been intentional to develop his life beyond his church and denomination by cultivating his relationship with his wife and adult children, gardening, continuing his involvement in a community service organization, and participating in spiritual direction training. For his own spiritual direction he meets with someone monthly in the Detroit area.

At a recent gathering of more than one thousand church leaders from the rust belt, Langley listened intently as one minister spoke of his dream to be part of a region he can be proud of. Those in attendance responded with deep, visceral agreement and committed themselves to serve as instruments of God in communities that are making the long-term transition from combustion to green technology. The group experienced consensus about the desire to bring evangelism and social justice together in their witness to God's loving rule on earth.[2]

7

Never Waste a Crisis

Learning from the Trouble That Comes

In *7 Lessons for Leading in Crisis*, management professor and former CEO Bill George credits Nicolò Machiavelli with the quote, "Never waste the opportunities offered by a good crisis." Translating this quote into the world of organizational leadership, George states, "Although it is hard to recognize at the time, crisis provides a unique opportunity to create trans-formative change in your organization."[1]

This insight matches up well with biblical faith. According to scripture, God not only strengthens us to persevere through crisis (1 Corinthians 10:13); God also acts in the midst of crisis to redeem it, turning it in a powerfully positive direction (Genesis 50:20; Romans 8:28; James 1:2–4). Consider the implications of this for you and your congregation. God wants to inject cre-ative meaning into your misfortune. Your crisis isn't just an unfortunate inter-ruption or inconvenient detour, and your goal isn't just to get back on track or return, as much as possible, to the way things were before. God intends to use your crisis to draw you further along toward your full potential as a partner in God's mission. Your goal is to look for lessons that will allow you to emerge from your crisis not only different–which is inevitable–but better.

Crisis and the Inevitability of Change–For Better or Worse

One of the definitions of *crisis* is "an unstable or crucial time or state of affairs in which a decisive change is impending."[2] We might as well be honest about it: crisis *always* brings change. For better or worse, those who go through crisis are never the same again. The question, then, isn't *whether* crisis will change things, but *how* crisis will change things. Leaders know better than to leave this to chance.

In chapter 2, I mentioned the often-referenced idea that the Chinese expression for crisis combines the idea of danger and opportunity. I also acknowledged University of Pennsylvania professor Victor Mair's observation that the Chinese idea of crisis accents the possibility of a highly undesirable outcome.[3] A real danger exists that crisis will change things for the worse. This, in fact, accounts for the anxiety that comes with crises. Crises threaten us physically, psychologically, relationally, and spiritually. They can put us in financial holes out of which it proves difficult to climb. They can harm people. They can leave ministries and relationships seriously damaged.

On the other hand, crises can become turning points for good. They can force us to reorient ourselves around core values and recommit ourselves to our true mission. They can create a sense of urgency to do things we've talked about doing for a long time. They can obliterate obstacles to innovation. They can pick us up, like a tornado lifts a house, and land us in a new world, with new problems and different possibilities.

Sometimes, we require a crisis to overcome our inertia. W. Edwards Deming, who is credited with launching the Total Quality Management Movement, became a key figure in Japan's economic turnaround after World War II. He introduced new management principles to their business leaders. Had it not been for the high sense of urgency prevailing in Japan at that time, these principles might never have been implemented. They required unprecedented levels of organizational commitment and discipline. The devastations of war created an atmosphere of willingness to do whatever it took to turn things around. His management principles took hold in corporate America during a later time of economic crisis, when the United States seemed to be losing its competitive edge in the global marketplace. Not surprisingly, Deming titled his essential book on the topic *Out of the Crisis.*[4]

How might your congregation's crisis create an atmosphere of willingness to follow God into new territory?

You Won't Mold What You Can't Melt

As was pointed out in the previous chapter, crises are time limited. Even if a congregation handles a crisis poorly, a point in time will come when things settle back down. Congregations eventually move toward a new normal and get on with life.

This makes it all the more important that leaders lead with purpose through the unsettling days of intense trouble. The goal of crisis leadership isn't just organizational survival; it is ongoing growth toward the congregation's full potential in Christ. Crises actually present a unique opportunity for healthy congregational transformation.

One of my friends in ministry uses the three states of H_2O to illustrate the art of leadership. H_2O has three states: (1) ice, (2) water, and (3) steam. In its own way, so does an organization. An organization can get frozen, like ice; that is, it can rigidify into a particular way of doing things and become resistant to change. An organization can also heat up too much and boil over, like steam; that is, anxiety and anger can get out of control. The optimal situation for an organization is a balance between stability and fluidity, with programs and ministries–like sheets of ice floating on water– solidly in place but flexible, depending on the needs of the time. The art of leadership is knowing when to heat things up and when to cool things down to strike the right balance between continuity and change.

Consider the application of this for congregations that experience crisis. Crises heat congregations up to the boiling point. The initial challenge of leadership is to cool things down. Churches that heat up too much face real dangers–loss of vision and hope, chronic grief and conflict, loss of members, loss of financial support, and in extreme cases congregational demise. Leaders help their churches deal with whatever overheats them. Leaders help restore order, preserve vision, and sustain faith, hope, and love.

At the same time, leaders guard against cooling things down too quickly or too much. The impulse toward normality is almost irresistible, but wise churches balance this impulse with ongoing openness to development. Crises, properly managed, can facilitate a more fluid state within which congregations can discern and respond to God's nudging toward renewal and ongoing transformation. Crises provide a built-in opportunity to leverage the sense of urgency that crises create.

Learning and the Spiritual Development of People

Before getting into learning at the organization-wide level, let's highlight the very personal application of this possibility. As a leader, you will influence how others mature spiritually as a result of your congregation's crisis. Though unwelcome and unwanted, crises open a window of opportunity for personal learning and development. As the apostle Paul put in Romans, "We also boast in our sufferings, knowing that suffering produces endurance, and endurance produces character, and character produces hope" (Romans 5:3–4).

In an article entitled, "Don't Waste a Crisis,"[5] pastor and best-selling author John Ortberg concentrates on this dimension of crisis learning. He launches his article by referring to a survey he once participated in on spiritual formation. The survey's striking discovery concerned the number-one contributor to spiritual growth. When survey results came in, the most frequently credited impetus for growth wasn't transformational teaching or being in a small group or reading deep books or participating in energized worship or serving others. The greatest impetus to growth was suffering.

This doesn't mean that suffering itself guarantees growth. Writes Ortberg, "Crisis can lead to soul strength, but not if the soul is starved of other nutrients, and not apart from certain responses."[6] The support systems around those suffering and the personal choices made in response to the circumstances spelled the difference between those who buckled and those who grew.

Those of us who count on spoken and written word as our principal modes of influence will benefit from a reminder that our greatest influence may come from the safety net of understanding and encouragement we create for those in pain. We will certainly have things to say to inspire faith, hope, and love. After all, our leadership puts us in a position to address people's concerns in a public way. Still, our nonanxious presence[7] usually matters more than our words, as does our ability to help people draw on their internal and external resources to cope.

What kind of congregational environment best supports healthy spiritual development in response to crisis? Let me suggest the following ingredients as a starting point for consideration. People in crisis learn and grow best in a setting in which

- *faith and hope thrive.* Individuals' faith may be shaken by crisis, but their faith will be heartened if they are in the company of those who remain undaunted. The key here is that faith and hope are being modeled in purposeful recovery and spontaneous expressions of confidence, rather than being forced down people's throats.
- *love expresses itself as nonanxious presence.* In healthy holding environments people know that their primary gift to people in pain is faithful presence. They don't run from hurting people or try to fix everything or attempt answers to every question. They love, while leaving space within which each person can do the personal work that leads to healing and growth.
- *a spiritual formation mind-set prevails.* Surrounded by others who look opportunistically at the learning opportunities of daily life, people in crisis are more likely to look at their pain for personal development.
- *the fellowship functions as a mutually supportive learning community.* In crisis, isolation is dangerous. In contrast, we gain enormous encouragement and strength from being in the company of fellow strugglers. There we can share our pain and confusion without fear of judgment, and we can find our way together.

As mentioned in chapter 5, pastoral care in crisis should be designed to empower rather than simply protect. While remaining prepared for interventions with those who are overwhelmed by crisis, our primary task is to support people's intrinsic motivation to triumph over adversity. Pull your leadership team together. Make sure they are using their influence to promote the kind of environment within which people grow best. Have conversations with your small group leaders (Sunday school teachers, discipleship group leaders, home church facilitators, ministry team coordinators, or whatever your structure for group life may be) and reinforce the patterns of leadership that will most likely support people's spiritual growth.

To the degree that we speak and teach, our best service comes in the form of questions:

- How is God using this experience to produce more of the fruit of the Spirit in you? (Galatians 5:22–23) How is this experience making you more loving, joyful, peaceable, patient, kind, good, faithful and faith-filled, gentle, and self-controlled?
- How, to apply the wisdom of the apostle Paul in Romans, is this experience producing perseverance, character, and hope? (Romans 5:3–5)

While you're asking these questions of others, don't forget to ask them of yourself too!

Learning about Crisis Itself

Moving from personal development to congregational development, the first level at which your congregation can learn from crisis has to do with managing crises in the future. Drawing on your fresh experience as well as the records you accumulated during your crisis recovery process, you and your fellow congregational leaders can get in front of the potential crises of tomorrow.

The authors of *Crisis Management: Master the Skills to Prevent Disasters* provide a list of questions for postcrisis reflection:

- Given what we knew at the time, could the crisis have been avoided? How?
- What were the early warning signs of crisis?
- Could we have recognized the signs earlier? How?
- Which warning signals were ignored? Which were heeded?
- At what point did we realize that we faced a crisis?
- To what extent were we prepared with contingency plans or a crisis team?
- Did we have a solid plan, or did we rely on improvisation?
- Did we have the right people on the team? If not, who should have been included?
- What was the nature of our communications to different audiences? How effective were those communications?
- How effective was our public spokesperson?

- Was our leadership highly visible?
- Were our responses timely and adequate for the situation?
- What did we do right? What could we have done better?
- Which were our biggest mistakes?
- Knowing what we know now, how can we prevent the same type of crisis from occurring again?
- And the ultimate question: If we could replay this entire event, what would we do differently?[8]

Manage Your Fears While You Manage Your Risks

This kind of postcrisis reflection has to do with risk management, which has become a major industry. Its influence has crossed over from business to faith-based organizations. At the back of this book you will find a list of organizations and resources devoted to crisis prevention and preparation. The field is growing rapidly, as more and more congregations come to terms with the dangers of doing business.

In the next chapter, we will take a closer look at what congregations can do about potential catastrophes before they occur. For now, let's consider a complication that can occur when the planning and prevention mind-set takes hold in the aftermath of a crisis. Traumatized by tragedy, we find ourselves saying, "This must never happen again." We pour our energy into barricading the congregation against future threats.

Some of this is necessary, as the next chapter will address. Nevertheless, the danger lurks that prudent planning will become an anxious obsession that locks in a congregation's missional energy while locking out danger. Dr. Al Meredith recognized this danger when leading Wedgwood Baptist Church beyond its tragic encounter with a gunman. The church took simple precautions to put people more at ease. Meredith also reminded people that "there's not enough money to screen people and hire security at church . . . We simply can't remove all risk. Ultimately, our only security is in Christ." His church has an administrative committee that deals with risk management. At the same time, they have refused to let a security mind-set overtake the missional mind-set.

During my days as Pastor of Holmeswood Baptist Church in Kansas City, we found ourselves having to deal with break-ins and vandalism. I remember the occasion when leaders met to discuss the problem of neighborhood kids who had figured out how to get into our church gym after hours. They placed a rock under the back door that was just big enough to prevent the door from locking.

The conversation centered on how better to secure the building, until one of the leaders at the table asked a question we hadn't thought to ask. "When the neighborhood kids get into the gym, are they causing any damage?" "Well, no," came the answer. "Then why don't we see this as a ministry opportunity rather than as a problem? Rather than getting better at locking them out, let's figure out how to welcome them in."

A new ministry developed as a result of that conversation. The leader who raised the fresh question led the way. He gathered a group of interested members and launched a neighborhood basketball program, with one night devoted to school-age students and another night devoted to adults, mostly young men. Not only did the program meet a neighborhood need and open the door to friendship and faith sharing, it produced another, unexpected benefit: the vandalism that had been occurring with increased frequency suddenly stopped.

Consider other ways churches can overcompensate in the aftermath of crisis:

- Personnel crises can lead to unnecessary and even irksome policies, creating a more unpleasant working environment and making it more difficult to hire and/or retain quality staff.
- Financial exigency can lead to policies and practices that linger well past the resolution of the crisis, making it frustrating for ministry leaders to gain access to the budgeted funds that make their work possible.
- Security-related crises can lead to a fortress mentality that becomes paranoid and inhospitable.
- Crises born of human failure and sin can send the roots of pain deep into the soul of a congregation, creating a culture of distrust that proves self-fulfilling and self-defeating.
- An accident, like First Baptist Church Shreveport's bus accident, can have a chilling effect on planning and participation levels with future church-sponsored trips.

When anxiety gets in the congregational driver's seat, missional passion gets hijacked by administrative control. As George Bullard points out, this becomes a recipe for congregational stagnation and decline. Vision belongs in the driver's seat, with management in the back seat providing a supportive role.[9]

A teachable congregation will harvest learnings from a crisis situation and develop plans to avoid, mitigate, and resolve future crises–you certainly don't want the same thing to happen again. At the same time you want to remain driven by God-given vision not fear!

Learning and Missional Alignment

Crisis affords you an opportunity not only to manage your congregation's ongoing risks more effectively; it also affords you an opportunity to strengthen alignment with the congregation's existing mission, vision, and values. Crises have a way of highlighting how we're getting things right. We can point to these in ways that reinforce healthy habits. Crises also have a way of exposing how we've drifted. We can use the crisis as a teachable moment to promote a stronger congruence between the things we say we believe and the way we actually behave.

First Baptist Shreveport's involvement with disaster relief in the aftermath of Hurricane Katrina in 2005 became an object lesson to reinforce our congregation's development as an externally focused rather than an internally focused church. By means of personal involvement, the pulpit, writing, and other interactions with members, I emphasized how our service in the city reflected the spirit God was cultivating in us. Other congregational leaders picked up on this message and reinforced it in their spheres of congregational influence. Our goal wasn't to pat ourselves on the back. Our goal was to make our congregation more mindful about what our God-given calling looked like in real life. This could motivate us toward more of the same.

By their very nature, mission, vision, and values have an aspirational quality about them. They hold up a possibility that lies beyond our current reach. They beckon, inspiring us to close the gap between who or where we are and who or where God wants us to be.

Crises provide a midcourse exam for how we're doing on the journey, and they provide us with a unique opportunity to push past obstacles that have stood in our way. The people of Sandy Run Baptist Church, for instance, can look back from this side of their crisis and admit that the sanctuary fire liberated them from overattachment to their historic building. It reconnected them to the vital conviction that church is not a place; it's a people. In the aftermath of the fire they adopted the slogan, "The building has burned, but the church is still alive!" This slogan continues to remind them of what has enduring value and what doesn't. They know that they need to be reminded of it more than ever, now that they are back on campus in beautiful, modernized facilities.

As mentioned earlier, New Horizon Christian Church in Akron, Ohio, got unstuck about worship as a result of relocating to the basement-level fellowship hall during replacement of leaking pipes under the sanctuary. Pastor Jim Bane used the necessities of the moment—out of the sanctuary, no pipe organ, no pews, no favorite seating locations—to rearrange the worship space, alter the level of formality, and lead the church to reflect more deeply on the true nature of worship. "There's something about being displaced," says Bane, "that makes you more thoughtful."

New Life Church in Colorado Springs reinforced its commitments to worship, prayer, and small groups as a result of its crises—not because these had faded in strength, but just the opposite. Contrary to what many outsiders expected, the church weathered the departure of its charismatic founding pastor because these aspects of the church remained strong. People were in the habit of fixing their eyes on Christ in worship rather than on a human leader. They had small-group-related peer relationships as a center of energy for fellowship and ministry. Their deeply embedded culture of prayer became a source of great purpose, strength, and encouragement. These same strengths came into play again after the trauma of a murderous gunman. In the aftermath of these crises, Pastor Boyd and other congregational leaders called attention to the role these healthy commitments played in New Life's resiliency, thus solidifying these as vital, core commitments.

The opportunity for strengthening missional alignment as a consequence of crisis can come into play at any level of the congregation's life. For the church whose treasurer embezzled nearly $500,000 of its capital funds and then committed suicide when his malfeasance was discovered, crisis brought a renewal of commitment to healthy relationships. Says the pastor, "It heightened our sense of compassion. Petty squabbles vanished." The dos and don'ts of healthy relationship are one thing when dealt with during Bible study in a Sunday school class; they're quite another when they come into play in the dramatic developments of the church. Wise congregational leaders look for teachable moments wherever they can find them, recognizing the classroom potential in every corner of the congregation's life.

Learning and Response to Emerging Vision

Teachable congregations will use crisis as an opportunity to improve their management of risk. They will become more closely aligned in actual practice with the mission, vision, and values they affirm. Teachable congregations will also discover within their crises the seeds of new ministry. They will come out on the back side of crisis with fresh perspective for fulfilling their calling in Christ.

In keeping with an old saying about necessity, crisis can become "the mother of missional invention." Consider the featured congregational story that precedes this chapter. Pastor Danny Langley and other thoughtful leaders of Crosspointe Meadows Church in metro Detroit had the presence of mind to think missionally as they led the congregation forward. They asked not only what they could do to cut costs but also how they could reinvent themselves to fulfill their mission under strikingly new circumstances. They committed themselves to serve members and those in the community who were struggling to make ends meet. Their money ministry is actually one part of a multifaceted "20/20 Strategy," focused on serving people who live within a twenty-block, twenty-mile radius in every direction from the church. Their innovative approach to partnering with an existing ministry to Japanese and other Asians in the community is another expression of this larger strategy.

The future may bring additional innovation. Langley admits that he had not, until recently, given serious thought about the church's role in creating business opportunities for the unemployed and thereby participating in the economic renewal of the region. He expresses appreciation to some of his African American colleagues for demonstrating how this works. Says Langley, "This is a social justice issue that is integral to the gospel."

As the Crosspointe Meadows story shows, crises introduce new avenues of ministry even as they block off existing ones. If we're open to it, God will get the upper hand on misfortune and thrust us into new, creative territory. Clearly, a healthy church isn't just about carefully orchestrated strategic planning and execution. It's also about openness to the wind of the Spirit, who can blow us in directions we hadn't anticipated.

Failing Forward

For real learning to occur in the aftermath of crisis, not only do we need to pinpoint the things we've done right and the opportunities that have emerged from crisis; we also need to reflect on mistakes we've made leading up to and following the eruption of crisis. This isn't easy work.

It helps if we've cultivated a culture of grace, with permission to fail and learn from mistakes. Even if we haven't, we can use this occasion to affirm the importance of this value and put it to good use. We don't have to ignore or wallow in failure. We can, to borrow the title of a book by former pastor and best-selling author John Maxwell, commit ourselves to "failing forward."[10]

The leaders of University Baptist Church of Waco have acknowledged that they didn't communicate as well as they should have after Kyle Lake's death. They didn't provide adequate forums for congregational input about the future of the church. They didn't work at congregational buy-in before hiring a second community pastor or calling a new teaching pastor. They've learned from these mistakes and now have the experience as a reference point for future decision making. Kyle's successor, Josh Carney, actually encouraged the elders to call a town hall meeting shortly after his arrival to dialogue with the congregation about how the decision-making process had gone. It went a long way toward clearing the air and easing Josh's transition into his role.

In counseling sessions for New Life of Colorado Springs, when members dealing with the trauma of a shooter on campus consistently turned their conversations toward Ted Haggard's departure, congregational leaders realized that they hadn't adequately facilitated emotional healing related to that earlier crisis. Rather than dodge accountability, they accepted responsibility and acknowledged their oversight. They supported new pastor Brady Boyd's initiatives to facilitate healthier healing the second time around.

The leaders of these congregations acknowledged their mistakes and learned from their failures. Every church can benefit from their example. I like the way the Living Bible has paraphrased Proverbs 28:13: "A man who refuses to admit his mistakes can never be successful. But if he confesses and forsakes them, he gets another chance" (Proverbs 28:13, TLB).

Progress is the goal of postcrisis reflection, not perfection; so don't waste time in an atmosphere of cover-up or recrimination. Put everything on the table and deal with it, squeezing every ounce of learning from it that you can. If you will, your mistakes can become your friends. God will not let a single one of them go to waste.

Facilitating Congregational Learning

Crisis-related learning can occur in any number of settings and take shape in any number of ways. The goal is that everyone will engage in crisis-related learning.

Without a doubt, you will want to formalize the process with key leaders, starting with the crisis management team itself. Depending on your congregation's structure and size, you will also have a board, a church council, a body of deacons, a pastoral team, or some other key leadership group to whom the congregation looks for direction. These groups play a particularly important role in postcrisis review and forward-aimed planning.

You may, depending on the circumstances, create a project-based team to facilitate learning and development. After the sudden resignation of its pastor and three other staff members in September 2001, First Baptist Shreveport formed a transition team. With the support of a paid congregational coach, the church worked through issues that had led to its crisis. By the end of the multimonth process, they had taken action to resolve conflict, restore relationships, and rally around a new set of goals for the years ahead. This put the congregation in a better position to call a pastor whose vision and passion matched the congregation's sense of where God was leading them. The pastor they called was me.

Beyond these formal groups and the orchestrated learning that can occur in such settings, the opportunities for learning are limited only by your imagination. The pulpit, the pen, town hall gatherings, small group discussions, focus groups, surveys, pastoral visits, parking lot conversations, e-mail—any of these can provide opportunities for interaction and insight . . . as long as they're channeled in a constructive way. You will want to provide appropriate venues for shared learning to keep it from spilling out in counterproductive ways and so that lessons are captured for timely and effective application.

By all means, make sure that the conversation is multidirectional. You will be not only the teacher but also the learner. You and everyone else will benefit from multiple points of view. First and foremost, make sure that the learning experience is centered in prayer. After all, the point of view that matters most is God's point of view. As learners, you will be listening for God's redemptive insight and direction.

Becoming a Learning Organization

God wants you to look at your crisis as a teachable moment. More than that, God wants the teachable spirit to permeate your congregation at all times. Peter Senge popularized the idea of "the learning organization," an organization where "people expand their capacity to create the results they truly desire, where new and expansive patterns of thinking are nurtured, where collective aspiration is set free, and where people are continually learning how to learn together."[11] This idea serves congregations well as they work their way through crisis and beyond. Not only can you learn from your crisis and move further in the direction of your full potential in Christ, you can use this teachable moment to make the shared-learning mind-set a permanent part of your congregation's repertoire.

Reflection Questions

Reflect personally on the following questions. If you are using this book with a study group, share your perspectives with each other. If you aren't currently experiencing a congregational crisis, think of a crisis your congregation has experienced or might experience and project yourself into that situation when reflecting on the questions.

- In what ways might individuals be shaped spiritually through the experience of congregational crisis? What are you doing to facilitate this potential?
- What have you learned so far from the way your congregation has handled the crisis? What did you do right? What might you do differently next time?
- How might God be using your circumstances as a congregation to strengthen your alignment with your God-given mission, vision, and values? What new possibilities are emerging?

Congregations in Focus

Congregational United Church of Christ, Punta Gorda, Florida

The people of Punta Gorda, Florida, can be forgiven for consider-ing Friday the thirteenth an unlucky day. That's the day in August 2004 when Hurricane Charley swept through town with category 4 to 5 winds and gusts of over 175 miles per hour, leaving homes, businesses, and community infrastructures devastated. In the larger Charlotte County area, eleven thousand dwellings were damaged beyond repair. Six school buildings had to be rebuilt. Four people lost their lives.

For Bill Klossner, pastor of Punta Gorda's Congregational United Church of Christ (CUCC), and other leaders of the community, Hurri-cane Charley presented a mountainous challenge. How do you rebuild a town, an economy, and the spirit of the people?

Given the time of year and the seasonal nature of the population, many of the homes sat empty. Bill estimates that only 25–30 percent of his congregation were in town. Eighty percent of his leadership was elsewhere. Until the church's moderator and the church's treasurer returned to town four days after the destruction, Bill piloted the church's response largely on his own. Fortunately, congregational trust ran high. Members didn't have time to micromanage things, given that they had their own personal property damage with which to contend. These circumstances allowed a small team of decision makers to act with dispatch.

Storm damage greatly complicated communications in the days immediately following the hurricane. It took five days for electrical power to return to the church. Bill had to drive about a mile out of town to use his cell phone. The church allowed Verizon to set up a mobile tower on its parking lot about one week into the crisis. Once Bill had Internet capabilities again, he began providing regular e-mail updates to members and others who were interested to know how things were going.

Decisions couldn't wait. The day after the hurricane struck, Bill had his first conversation with an insurance adjuster, who came the following Friday to assess damage to the church structure. Repairs cost just under $500,000. Through a friend, Bill was able to arrange for a roofing crew to come quickly. On a single Saturday, the crew had the job done. Meanwhile, a professional drying company came from Michigan and dried out the church for nine days. This rapid response spared the church the problem of mold, which often creates as many problems as the original damage.

On Sunday, August 15, two days after the hurricane, seven members gathered outside the church and worshiped. Bill had no need to change the title of his message—"When Trouble Comes"—which had been planned before the storm. For the three Sundays following, the congregation worshiped in makeshift locations in the facility. After that, the congregation worshiped in the sanctuary, with crews removing the scaffolding each weekend until they completed the renovations. This reflected a strategic leadership decision to provide members with some stability in the midst of a disruptive time of their lives.

The fellowship hall had to be stripped down to the cement block. The office suffered only ceiling tile damage, which allowed Bill and others to continue using it through the renovation process. Thanks to great working relationships with the claims adjuster and the contractor, CUCC had its facilities fully restored by April 2005, perhaps the first church in the area to get this done. Some churches in the area took multiple years to accomplish this, struggling through church decision-making processes and difficulties with claims adjusters and contractors.

"There's an irony in a process like this," says Klossner. "When you slow down decision making, members lose trust and experience more discouragement." At a debriefing provided for affected pastors by the United Church of Christ's National Disaster Coordinator, Bill got confirmation of this from other pastors. He counts himself blessed that the church was able to expedite the crisis recovery process without conflict. The church empowered a committee of five to make all the decisions, even when it came to changing interior color schemes and selecting replacement furnishings, like softer new chairs.

The congregation covered the cost of renovations without difficulty, thanks to an up-to-date property insurance policy, a preexisting capital fund, and generous gifts from churches in thirteen different United Church of Christ (UCC) conferences. In addition to monetary support, CUCC received a wave of prayer and goodwill from churches and Sunday school classes from as far away as Maryland, Illinois, and

Iowa. Some members even developed pen pal relationships with those who wrote to express concern.

Crises like this one can be tough on congregational leaders. At the denominational debriefing, Bill learned about a study related to Hurricane Andrew indicating that 75 percent of clergy serving in the hardest-hit area before that 1992 hurricane had left their church in the year following. Ninety-five percent of that group had left ministry all together. Based on his own experience, Bill understood why the crisis of a hurricane could take such a leadership toll. He carried not only the concerns of the church and community with him but also concerns related to his own damaged home. Thankfully, the damage to his home was such that he and his wife decided to postpone most of the repairs until the church had completed its work. Furthermore, his having already served the congregation for sixteen years prior to the hurricane provided a basis of stability and trust that eased the anxiety of everyone concerned.

Bill's deep roots in the church and community allowed him to extend the reach of his care, as confidant to city leaders and as chaplain to the Punta Gorda Police Department. He also had opportunities beyond the community, traveling to New Orleans in the aftermath of Hurricane Katrina to encourage pastors there. That trip, some fifteen months after Hurricane Charley, proved cathartic. Seeing all the damage along the road between Biloxi, Mississippi, and New Orleans, he experienced something of a delayed emotional reaction to what his community and he had experienced the year before. He realized that the challenges of living and pastoring through crisis had affected him more deeply than he thought.

Punta Gorda has experienced what Klossner calls "urban renewal by natural disaster." Civic leaders engaged the community in a master planning process that went extremely well. The process has invigorated the community and led to a wave of fresh construction, including two new hotels, a new event center, and six new schools in the school district, four of them in Punta Gorda itself.

CUCC has experienced its own version of the storm's silver lining. The congregation hasn't changed its mission as an open, welcoming place where people can explore faith. It has helped the congregation see how crisis can strengthen these values, propelling it more intentionally than ever into the community. The church is now more externally focused than it was before.

Klossner affirms the biblical truth of Romans 8:28: "In all things God works for the good of those who love him, who have been called according to his purpose." Reflecting back on his experience, he now says with more confidence than ever that "good things can come out of a crisis."

8

Getting in Front of Crisis

Prevention and Preparation

On October 1, 2010, a Tampa, Florida jury awarded $5 million to a young man who suffered severe injuries on a 2003 ski trip hosted by Idlewild Baptist Church, Lutz, Florida. The mother was deemed responsible for 5 percent of the damages, while the church was deemed responsible for 95 percent–$4.75 million.

The plaintiff, fourteen years old at the time of the accident, had never skied before. According to trial testimony, his mother received assurances that he would get instruction before going out on the slopes on his own. She also was told that the church would provide one chaperone for every ten minors. As it turned out, the plaintiff received neither instruction nor supervision. Alone on the slopes, he became disoriented and ended up on an expert slope, where he crashed into another skier at approximately fifty-five miles per hour, suffering spinal fractures and permanent nerve damage to his left leg.

Idlewild Baptist Church immediately announced its intentions to contest the verdict. Said Brian McDougall, executive associate pastor of the eleven-thousand-member congregation,

> We do not agree with the verdict and know that important evidence was not heard by the jury. Idlewild has always maintained the highest safety standards in all our church activities. We have had thousands of people travel safely with us on hundreds of trips without an issue of this nature.[1]

Whatever the final outcome of the legal proceedings related to this unfortunate accident, we can all agree that the story highlights our vulnerability and our accountability as churches. It raises the question: Are we doing all we can to prevent preventable crises and prepare for those that might occur anyway?

Be Prepared

"Be prepared." That's the well-known Boy Scouts motto, a reminder that though we can't control the future completely or even predict it with absolute certainty, we can ready ourselves for it and even influence it through proactive planning and action.

If you've led your congregation through a crisis, you don't need a story like the Idlewild story to be sold on the value of preparation. Looking back on your crisis, you can find your own evidence of how readiness factored into the way your crisis unfolded. You were prepared in some ways. These dimensions of readiness strengthened your response and recovery. In some ways you weren't prepared. These vulnerabilities complicated your response and recovery.

The purpose here isn't to criticize or applaud your congregation's level of readiness for a previous crisis. The purpose is to use experience as an inducement for what happens next. No matter how well or how poorly you prepared for your last crisis, you can take steps to avoid avoidable crises in the future and prepare for those that may occur anyway. You can build risk-management thinking into your congregation's strategic tool box.

Dealing with Resistance to Risk Management

You may have to deal with resistance to this kind of planning before you get started. That resistance can originate in more than one concern. Some congregations fear that a focus on risk management will foster a fortress mentality. This runs contrary to the missional mind-set we actually want to cultivate, and we certainly do want to guard against obsessive risk avoidance. The truth, however, is that proactive planning can have the opposite effect. If people have confidence about the congregation's level of preparedness, they can turn their attention to other things. This kind of planning, properly done, builds confidence not fear.

Denial is another hurdle you and your congregation will leap in order to do proactive planning. You simply can't give in to the notion that "it won't happen here." Yet that's precisely what happens every day in congregations across North America. Not having suffered a particular kind of crisis in the past, they fail to consider that the past is no predictor of the future. Either they overestimate their current level of readiness or they think themselves immune. Failing to prepare or failing to test their readiness, they leave their future unnecessarily to chance.

Supporting the appeal of denial is our built-in resistance to the costs of prevention and preparation. This kind of planning and action costs time, attention, and money. It can be inconvenient, given other things on which we prefer to focus, and it forces us to monkey around with the status quo, which can cause resistance. I remember, for instance, the push-back we got in one of the congregations I pastored when we decided to regain control of access to the church building. It necessitated that we ask everyone with a key to the church to turn in their keys. You would have thought we had taken away their driving privileges!

In an online article about crisis planning, reputation management consultant Bill Patterson confronts corporate leaders with yet another factor that thwarts crisis planning: their overconfidence in themselves as leaders under pressure:

> Most of us like to think we do our best work in the midst of a crisis or controversy, when the adrenaline is flowing and we can make vital decisions in a split second. And in fact, many executives do perform extremely well under pressure . . . But in a world when the wrong split-second decision can cost a company millions in negative publicity, not being prepared is not worth the risk–to executives or the companies they work for.[2]

Though Patterson aims his warning at corporate executives, those of us in congregational leadership positions can apply the truth of his statements to ourselves. If we perform well under pressure, we may be tempted to trust our instincts should crises come. We owe it to our churches to think otherwise. Not only do crises put dollars and reputation at stake–as Patterson points out–they put lives at stake and they impact the congregation's ongoing mission.

Even in congregations with a thoughtful, forward-looking focus, the danger remains that we will concentrate on upside potential and neglect downside vulnerabilities and threats. Smart are the congregations that include crisis-related risk assessment in their review of their strengths, weaknesses, opportunities, and threats (SWOT analysis). Smarter still are the congregations that then follow up that analysis with planning and preparation against the risks they identify.

The Goals of Risk Management

Risk management aims at two goals: *prevention* and *preparation.* You want to prevent preventable disasters and prepare for those that might occur anyway.

Prevention

Even if most congregations could do more, every congregation I know has some measure of prevention planning in its system. For instance, it has become standard practice for congregations to have policies for handling contributions, and an ever-growing number of congregations have child-protection policies for workers with minors. These are but two examples of proactive planning. Why do provisions like these exist? Clearly, these policies and practices aim to avoid avoidable problems, built on awareness that the best way to deal with a crisis is to keep it from happening in the first place. Untold numbers of crises have been averted altogether because of proactive planning.

I'd tell you a story at this point, but how do you tell the story of something that didn't occur? How do you tell the story of a potential embezzler who never got a chance to steal funds from the church because a transfer of funds from one account to another required two signatures? How do you tell the story of child abuse that never occurred because two adults must always be present during youth and children programming? Where's the newspaper headline for a church that honors copyright laws in its copying practices and therefore hasn't had to deal with a damaging lawsuit? In these and hundreds of other ways, proactive congregations steer clear of disasters that otherwise lie in wait. But the issue isn't whether we're doing something related to crisis prevention. The issue is whether we're doing enough. Are we properly stewarding our responsibility to prevent preventable crises? What avoidable risks remain untended?

Preparation

Even with careful planning, some crises still occur. First Baptist Shreveport's bus accident didn't happen because of neglect on the part of those preparing for the trip. In keeping with trip preparation policies, the bus—less than two years old and with limited wear and tear—was fully inspected and serviced. All drivers were trained and certified. Still, the accident occurred.

By proactive planning we can reduce the likelihood of trouble, but we can't eliminate risk altogether. That's why we need not only prevention plans but preparation plans as well. We need to do contingency planning so that should a crisis occur, we will be in a better position to respond and recover effectively.

In some cases, we can't do anything to prevent a crisis; all we can do is prepare. I immediately think of the tornadoes that ravaged multiple communities in the United States in the spring of 2011. One of those communities, Joplin, Missouri, lost more than 150 lives and suffered an estimated $3 billion in damage on Sunday, May 22, when a multiple-vortex tornado swept through the center of town. Not even the finest meteorologists could have predicted the historic strength of that twister. Certainly no one pretends that anything could have been done to stop it. Nonetheless, preparation made a difference. The tornado warning system gave residents twenty-four minutes' notice to find safe shelter. Doctors and nurses at St. John's Regional Medical Center, who had practiced tornado drills for years, got patients away from windows, closed blinds, and activated emergency generators. Trained public service providers—police, firefighters, medics, and others—knew what to do once the tornado struck, making their way through the dark and the rain to rescue the trapped and aid the wounded. Skilled and experienced disaster relief teams descended on the city just as quickly to assist with victim support and cleanup. This is but a sampling of the concerted effort that came into play immediately before and after the tornado, thanks to prepared people in the public and private sectors. Preparation didn't give Joplin disaster immunity, but it did save lives and enhance the capacity of the community to respond and recover.

When your congregation experiences crisis, preparation provides the foundation on which you and the rest of the congregation will build your response. Preparation makes you more agile. It facilitates your ability to react in a timely, effective, adaptive-dealing way.

A Word about Holistic Thinking

For many congregations, it takes a crisis—their own or someone else's—to spur them toward proactive planning related to their risks. That may be the case for you and your congregation. Just because a single issue has drawn you to planning doesn't mean that your planning has to have a single-issue focus. This chapter assumes that you will think about multiple risks and do more comprehensive planning. You may choose to tackle the issues one risk at a time, but at least you can have the larger perspective in mind as you do the work.

Form a Crisis Planning Team

The starting point for crisis prevention and preparation is the creation of a crisis planning team (some organizations prefer to call it a risk management team or a crisis action team). If you so choose, this team will do the planning now and coordinate crisis response later. If you have arrived at this point after a crisis, your crisis planning team may or may not comprise the same people who coordinated your crisis response.

If you're not in a position to create a separate crisis planning team, make sure you get this topic on the agenda of the group that serves as your congregation's core leadership group. What matters is that some group takes responsibility for being proactive about congregational risk.

It makes sense to keep the size of the core group manageable—you can always include additional participants in subgroups for risk-specific planning. If a crisis occurs, you will know of specialists who will be particularly helpful, depending on the nature of the crisis. They can join the team on an as-needed basis. A core group of five to nine members, depending on the size of your church and the availability of volunteers, works best.

Given that you will be dealing with such issues as the law, insurance, building and grounds, personnel, security, finances, communications, mental health, and information technology, it makes sense to look for people in your congregation who have expertise in these or other areas. Variety of perspective will produce more comprehensive and balanced planning.

Assess

Once formed, your crisis planning team will begin its work with risk assessment. This involves identifying potential risks, creating a priority list for further attention, and evaluating your present level of preparedness for incidents related to these risks.

Identify Potential Risks

Potential risks will vary from congregation to congregation. For instance, a church in tornado alley will have to deal with contingencies that churches in other regions won't. Churches with older facilities will have concerns different from those in newer facilities or those leasing their property. Those with a child development center, in comparison with those focused on services to senior adults, will have both similar and different risks with which to contend.

Churches in general share a set of risks related to the nature of the business. We deal with volunteerism in every ministry of the church, including sensitive areas like working with minors and handling money. One-on-one pastoral care and counseling occur regularly. We cultivate a culture of hospitality, intentionally welcoming strangers onto our campus and often assuming the best related to people's motives and mind-set. We sponsor mission trips, recreational outings, retreats, and other experiences involving church-sponsored travel. We resource our ministries with the charitable giving of members, relying on strong and stable giving from a core group of givers. These factors and many more will come into play as you assess your congregation's risks.

The crisis planning team will benefit from broad-based involvement at the assessment stage. Many minds are better than a few, so don't just depend on the input of this group. Get input from people in all the ministries of the church. Each ministry area will have a unique perspective and possibly see risk where others don't. First Baptist, Norman, Oklahoma, might never have purchased defibrillators, trained people to use them, and stationed them in multiple locations around the church, had it not been for leaders in the senior adult ministry who pointed out the need. When a beloved member had a heart attack during church services, one of those defibrillators, in the hands of a trained responder, saved his life.

Prioritize Risks

After you've identified your congregation's risks, prioritize them. You can do so based on two variables: probability and potential impact.

How probable is the risk? You may have listed hurricanes as a potential risk, but if your church is in Butte, Montana, your chances of being struck by a meteor are probably higher. On the other hand, if your congregation has a children's ministry, the risks of abuse or injury are real and constant. Sharpen your focus by identifying the crises most likely to occur.

With this narrowed list, ask yourselves the next question: If a crisis were to occur in these areas, which would have the greatest potential impact? Obviously, risks with the highest degree of probability and greatest potential impact belong at the top of the list. Those with a lower degree of probability and/or less potential impact can slip to the bottom. Ultimately the question is qualitative rather than quantitative. See if you can reach consensus as a group on your top ten. You can then zero in on these for further attention.

Do a Risk Audit

Once you have your top ten list, it's time to do a risk audit. Your purpose with a risk audit is to determine your congregation's current state of readiness to prevent or respond to each of your top risks. Have you taken responsible precautions to avoid the avoidable? Are you prepared should something unwelcome occur?

For leaders at The Church at Rock Creek, in Little Rock, Arkansas, news coverage about church shootings prompted them to take their risk management to a new level. Before all was said and done, they created a multifaceted emergency plan for their congregation.[3]

As it related to potential gun violence, they knew before planning began that they weren't adequately prepared to prevent it or respond should it occur on their campus. With four weekend services and an average attendance of four thousand, they knew they bore responsibility for the safety and wellbeing of a lot of people.

Based on information they found on the Internet, in state resources, and from conversations with their congregation's chief of security, they got a clearer picture of their current state of readiness. Sites like Churchsafety .com greatly simplified the process. Churchsafety.com provides free risk assessment questionnaires, feature articles, and fee-based planning resources on a full range of congregational risks. Here are Churchsafety.com's assessment questions related to gun violence:

- Do we have an emergency or crisis plan in place?
- Do we train our leadership, ushers, or greeters in crisis response?
- Do we train our ushers or greeters on how to respond to suspicious persons?
- Do we conduct regular evacuation or emergency response training?
- Have we identified key medical professionals in our congregation?
- Do we have quick access to phones at all times in key locations?
- Are exit routes clearly marked?
- Have we taken measures to secure our buildings with lighting, security cameras, and lockdown areas?
- Have we questioned the local police department on ways we can be

ready to defend our congregation if an intruder emerges during a service?

- Have we discussed the possibility of hiring a security guard for the church?[4]

When a congregation like Rock Creek uses an assessment tool like this one, it gives them a starting point for planning. They may be able to answer "yes" to some of the questions, which means they won't have to start from scratch when planning. They may have to answer "no" to other questions. This simply highlights areas needing attention. The question-naires themselves suggest aspects of preparedness that can be used as a beginning checklist for the next stage of the process.

Design

Once you have a clearer picture of your congregation's current state of preparedness, your team is ready to develop plans to reduce your risks and improve your response. You may even decide to subdivide the design work, adding specialists from your church and outside experts to the sub-groups. It makes sense, for instance, to consider doctors, nurses, or other medically trained personnel in design work related to medical emergencies.

The objective of the design phase isn't to create an exhaustive plan that accounts for everything that could possibly happen. That wouldn't be realistic. Every incident has its own idiosyncrasies; even with a plan, there will be elements of improvisation in your responses. The objective of the design phase is to give you a solid starting point for improvisation. You want a written plan that is detailed enough to provide you with basic strategies for avoiding and responding to the crises that are most likely to occur. You want something reliable and readily available to which you and other leaders can turn as the starting point and ongoing guide for response and recovery.

Designing for Prevention

In the face of potential crises, the first question to ask is, "What can we do to avoid or neutralize this as a source of future problems?" Do you screen volunteers with youth and children? Do you keep church vehicles properly maintained? Do you have adequate lighting inside and outside of your building? Is your church free of unnecessary fire hazards? Have you established responsible protocols for handling contributions? These are but a few of the areas in which prevention planning can happen.

Prevention planning at one church I know zeroed in on the need for campus cleanup. An accumulation of material at the back of the church created a fire hazard and blocked access into and out of the building. Improper use of the boiler room for storage created a further fire hazard that could be remedied easily. Another church I know decided to do something about access into its buildings, in light of the fact that it had more than a dozen exterior doors. During prevention planning it decided to channel people through one entrance during weekday business hours and install an electronic entry system for authorized people needing access to other parts of the facility.

Designing for Response

Given that we can't plan away all crises, the next question is, "What can we do to mitigate future problems that might arise?" For instance, does your congregation have a plan for facility evacuation in case of an emergency? Do you have a communication protocol for notifying key leaders when a crisis occurs? How will you communicate with your congregation during and after a critical incident? How will you handle the news media? Is your congregation adequately insured? On whom will you call for medical, legal, and mental-health support? These are the kinds of questions you will ask and answer as you plan for the unwelcome contingencies of a crisis.

One congregation I know prioritized planning in the area of finances. It already had a basic set of policies and practices in place. During comprehensive planning, it added three new elements to its financial plan. First, it committed itself to upgrade its computer hardware and software and add an on-site and off-site information backup system. Second, it established new standards for cash reserves that allowed for the leaner summer months. Third, it decided to secure lines of credit and authorizations to tap the line of credit as needed.

Triggering Events

As a part of this design work, you can clarify the kinds of triggering events that will launch things into response mode. How will your greeters know it's time to alert staff or security about a suspicious person? What financial threshold has to be crossed before activating emergency expense-management procedures? When will you call 9-1-1 or notify child protection services? Some of your triggering circumstances will be more obvious than others. The plan should make it as easy as possible for people to recognize a potential crisis as soon as possible and get a jump on it. The sooner the situation gets into the hands of those who can manage it, the better.

Crisis Response and Ministry Continuity

As you plan your congregation's response to critical incidents, make sure you think in terms of both your response to the crisis itself and what you will do to keep the congregation functioning during the recovery period. What if, like Sandy Run Baptist Church in Hampton, South Carolina, your congregation experiences a devastating fire? What will you do to deal with the immediate situation, and what will you do to keep worship, Bible study, and administrative processes going during your dislocation? Or, what if, like University Baptist Church in Waco, Texas, you suddenly lose your pastor or another key staff person? How will you handle the immediate situation, and what will you do to keep your congregation's ministries going during the interim between leaders?

Who's in Charge?

You need to establish clear lines of authority as a part of your plan. You don't want people wondering who's in charge when crisis erupts.

On March 30, 1981, when President Ronald Reagan suffered life-threatening injuries in an assassination attempt, confusion reigned as to who held the reigns of executive leadership. Vice president George H. W. Bush was in transit on Air Force II and temporarily out of communication. Secretary of State Alexander Haag stood before reporters at the White House and announced, "I'm in charge here," despite the fact that two others, the Speaker of the House of Representatives and the President Pro Tempore of the Senate stood second and third in the line of succession. In the face of immediate criticism, he clarified that he was merely talking about orchestrating things at the White House until the vice president was back on the scene. The confusion didn't last long; but this situation illustrates the urgent importance of clear authority during a crisis situation.

Who gets the call that a problem is brewing or has already erupted? Who has authority to put crisis response strategies into play? Who leads the response team? Who handles communication? If the designated leader isn't available, who steps in as first alternate? Make sure you don't leave things fuzzy about these matters.

Contact Sheet

Your crisis management plan should include a contact sheet clarifying whom to call in an emergency situation and how to reach them. It should also include all office, home, and cell phone numbers of everyone on the crisis management team, crisis counselors, legal counsel, and any insurance company you may rely on.

Crisis Messages

It's not a bad idea to consider what your first messages would be to the congregation and the public, depending on the nature of the crisis. As community pastor Ben Dudley learned after the death of University Baptist of Waco's teaching pastor, you won't necessarily have much time before reporters begin calling in the event of a crisis. The more carefully you can plan your comments ahead of time, the better able you will be to communicate responsibly and constructively under the pressures of the moment.

The idea here isn't to craft your full message, but rather to create message templates that you can customize. This gives you a chance to incorporate key elements into what the spokesman will say. This is also the time to anticipate the most likely and challenging questions that could be asked as a result of each crisis. Many businesses go so far as to identify the twenty worst questions they could be asked during any Q&A session with the press or public.[5]

Anticipate that the church's main telephone number will be the one people call first when seeking or providing information in the midst of a crisis. Make sure your plan includes clear guidance for those who will be answering the phone.

Outside Support System

Don't forget the availability of outside support when crafting your plans. You don't have to handle everything yourself. How will firefighters, police, emergency medical teams, or other public support systems come into play? When will your insurance agent or attorney get called into action? Do you have a list of mental-health professionals on whom you can call, and do you know when to call on their services? Will there be a role for sister churches or your denominational support system? What other service providers might come into play, depending on the nature and scope of the crisis?

Final Words about Design

Don't let perfectionism get the best of you. Remember that the goal isn't to think of everything, but to prepare yourselves in general terms for your greatest risks. Rather than following some arbitrary idea of what your completed plan should look like, create something that works for you. Some congregations will create an elaborate file of materials. Others will end up with something as simple as action outlines. Some will have both.

These suggestions for design provide a starting point for crisis planning. For additional support you can refer back to earlier chapters in this book, which provide perspectives on crisis response and recovery. You can also turn to one or more of the planning resources listed at the back of the book.

Implement

When all is said and done, a plan is only as good as its implementation. Be sure to develop crisis *capabilities,* not just plans.[6] This means communicating the plans to the church and gaining congregational support for aspects of the plan that require approval. It means chipping away systematically at prevention measures that need to be addressed. It means providing training to those who will come into play during an emergency.

The plans will need to get into the hands of everyone with responsibilities in the event of a critical incident, and the plans will need to be filed in readily accessible locations. Contingency arrangements will need to be made with outside support systems to clarify the nature of their support as needs arise.

To test your plans and keep them fresh, you will want to run simulation exercises on a periodic basis. Furthermore, don't take lightly your congregation's need to familiarize itself with what it will do in case of an emergency. A growing number of congregations, for instance, have incorporated periodic evacuation drills into their weekend gatherings. Once inaugurated, crisis planning should become a continuous process. Plans should be evaluated regularly and refined, as necessary.

The Church at Rock Creek conducts annual training for its staff, ushers, greeters, Sunday school leaders, and other volunteers. This training proved its value in 2010 when a tornado siren began sounding during Wednesday-night programming. In keeping with the emergency plan, a worship pastor and adult workers got children to a secure location in the inner part of the church, and others on campus made their way to safety as well.

As a part of its security plan, Rock Creek now has a paid security team of off-duty police officers, the majority of them in plain clothes. Arkansas has a concealed carry law, but members have been encouraged not to carry their guns on campus. Those who choose to do so anyway have been warned to keep them concealed, since the security people don't know members from strangers and have been instructed to shoot if someone draws a gun. Clearly, the implementation of crisis plans can be serious business.

Preparedness and Congregational Culture

To this point in the conversation about prevention and preparedness, we have confined our conversation to crisis-related planning itself. In truth, a congregation's ability to handle a crisis has as much to do with its faith and character as it does with its technical skills in an emergency. Its response to crisis will reflect its ability to draw on the presence and power of God's Spirit. Its overall vitality as a congregation will greatly influence whether it emerges from crisis enlarged or weakened. The best thing your congregation can do to prepare for crisis is to continue cultivating your core strengths as the people of God.

Does your congregation have a shared understanding of congregational health? Has it fixed its sights on ongoing development? There are some fine organizations[7] and resources[8] that get at this issue, but ultimately the privilege and responsibility lies with each congregation to define and cultivate a culture of health. As a congregational leader, you will play an instrumental role in this regard.

Church consultant George Bullard looks closely at congregational health and transformation and provides guidance for promoting continuous renewal and development. He focuses on ten areas of congregational life, encouraging generative dialogue about these areas as an entrée into congregational development that builds on strengths and develops readiness for congregational transition and change. Four of these areas form what he calls the DNA of a congregation's life cycle. Consider the degree to which these characteristics are true of your congregation:

1. *Visionary leadership.* Our congregation has a strong, clear, and passionate sense of our identity involving mission and purpose (who we are), our core values (what we believe or highly value), our vision (where

we are heading), and our spiritual strategic journey as a congregation (how we are getting there).

2. *Relationship experiences.* Our congregation is doing well at attracting people to a Christ-centric faith journey (evangelism) and at helping people who are connected with our congregation to be on an intentional and maturing Christ-centric faith journey (discipleship development). Among the results of the faith journey of people in our congregation is a deepening spirituality, the development of numerous new leaders, and a willingness by many people to get actively involved in congregational leadership positions and in places of ministry service within and beyond the congregation (lay mobilization).

3. *Programmatic emphases.* Our congregation has outstanding programs, ministries, and activities for which we are well known throughout our congregation and our geographic community or the target groups we serve. Our programs, ministries, and activities seem to be growing in numbers and quality. Our programs are meeting real, identified, spiritual, social, and emotional needs of people.

4. *Accountable management.* Our congregation has excellent, flexible management systems (teams, committees, councils, boards, leadership communities) that empower the future direction of our congregation rather than seeking to control the future direction. Decision making is open and responsive to congregational input. Finances are healthy and increasing each year. The management systems are supportive of the visionary leadership efforts by the pastor, staff, and congregational leadership.[9]

What would you say are the primary signs of congregational health, and what can you be doing as leaders to promote the health of your congregation? A general condition of health will enhance your congregation's ability to respond to a crisis constructively and creatively.

Reflection Questions

Reflect personally on the following questions. If you are using this book with a study group, share your perspectives with each other. If you aren't currently experiencing a congregational crisis, think of a crisis your congregation has experienced or might experience and project yourself into that situation when reflecting on the questions.

- What are your congregation's most probable and potentially serious risks?
- What is your congregation's current state of readiness related to these risks?
- What steps do you need to take to improve your congregation's state of readiness?

Congregations in Focus

Sandy Run Baptist Church, Hampton, South Carolina

Paul Reid, pastor of Sandy Run Baptist Church, Hampton, South Carolina, woke up in the darkness of early morning Sunday, November 4, 2007, and sat down under the light of a lamp for scripture reading and prayer. The sound of a crash somewhere outside interrupted his devotion, and stepping to a window of the pastorium he looked toward his church, the direction from which the sound seemed to come. What he saw didn't make sense immediately: a bright light emanated from the building. Then it dawned on him that the sanctuary was on fire.

The sound Reid had heard was the air-conditioning and heating unit crashing through the roof. As soon as he realized he was witnessing something real rather than a dream, he roused his wife and asked her to call 9-1-1. He then ran over to the building, hoping to salvage church records and his books, but a mere touch of one of the windows made it clear that he had better not try to enter.

A well-trained team of volunteers from the Hampton Fire Department responded quickly under the leadership, it so happened, of one of the church's deacons. They worked tirelessly and efficiently to control the damage. They managed to save the social hall, a 1998 addition to the church that had been built to code with a fire wall separating it from the rest of the church. Unfortunately, the core structure, built in 1904 with fat lighter pine, went up like a tinder box.

People from the church and the community gathered all morning at the church's softball field and consoled each other as they watched firefighters battle the blaze. Many of those watching the devastation came from families that belonged to Sandy Run for generations. They and those whose memories they cherished had been married, eulogized, and baptized there. Pastor Reid's first order of business was to provide pastoral care, supporting them in their grief and encouraging them with hope.

At 11 a.m. they worshiped even without a sanctuary, setting up a salvaged, soaked piano in front of the bleachers to accompany their prayer and praise. The pianist played the Doxology. They sang "Amazing Grace." They prayed for God's providence. They declared their intention to rebuild.

A boy from the church, who found a penny near one of the fire trucks, placed the penny in Pastor Reid's hands and said, "Put that in the building fund." His gift inspired others, with $18,000 donated that morning alone to fund reconstruction.

Plans for reconstruction fell into place quickly, as did arrangements for the continuity of ministry during reconstruction. A building steering committee was formed to oversee the project. Despite other alternatives, the church elected to stay on campus throughout the process. The undamaged social hall, already outfitted for sound and video, served as the worship center. The pastorium functioned as a Sunday school space for children. Two rented mobile units provided the balance of needed educational space. A generous local music store provided a used organ and a piano for as long as needed.

Early on, Reid made the decision to focus on pastoral ministry and vision leadership, resisting the temptation to micromanage the rebuilding process. It helped that the church had members with special expertise who could work on and with the building steering committee. It also helped that the church could fund the project without complications, thanks to full-replacement insurance coverage and an expeditious claims process.

On the pastoral care front, Reid focused on grieving with and encouraging church members through face time during hospital visits, nursing home visits, and a lot of time in homes. He also introduced an innovation, stationing his wife's recently purchased Chevy Suburban in front of the church as an early morning and late-afternoon office. With electricity supplied by a drop cord attached to a power converter, he had all the energy needed to use his laptop computer, do administrative work, and make himself available for drop-by visits, whatever the weather conditions.

Vision leadership became an important part of the church's response to the crisis. Fire, unwelcome though it was, cleared away any undue attachment to architecture that might have existed. Reid used the moment to reemphasize the biblical view of the church as a living body rather than just an institution or a place. He also pointed the congregation beyond itself in ministry and mission.

A forward-looking deacon chair and a strong women's missions organization served as strong allies in the effort to lead the congregation toward Christlike service beyond itself. On the backside of the crisis, the church has revamped its missions education program for children and youth and launched an English-as-a-second-language ministry that serves Hispanic and Asian communities in the area. A renewed focus on outreach has also occurred, which has led to an upturn in professions of faith and involvement in the church.

The crisis didn't fully resolve itself quickly. It took from November 2007 to March 2010 for the church to complete the process of redesign and reconstruction and move into its new space. Involvement levels held up well despite the disruptions. Monetary resources actually improved.

Under the leadership of an effective chairman, the building steering committee did a good job of balancing decisiveness and congregational decision making throughout the project. Though minor disagreements arose over allocation of space, trust levels in the process remained high, and members were pleased with what resulted. Says Reid, "In terms of our facilities, it has propelled us out of the nineteenth century and into the twenty-first century."

Now that Sandy Run has an attractive, new home base for ministry, Reid sees the challenge as resisting the temptation to grow "at ease in Zion," an allusion to God's warning against complacency in Amos (Amos 6:1). The church has incorporated the symbol of the cross into the design of its church windows as a reminder, and members have a story from their conflagration to reinforce their memory.

A wooden cross had been put up outside the sanctuary for Lenten season, months before the fire. Still in place at the time of the fire, the cross survived the blaze. Members of the church and the media took photos of the cross silhouetted against the burning sanctuary. The image became a metaphor for the resilient strength of the cross and the self-giving way of Christ. At the groundbreaking ceremony, a large area was roped off in the shape of a cross, and members filled the space, shovels in hand, as a photographer captured the moment from a basket crane high above the proceedings.

Ask members of Sandy Run Baptist Church and they will tell you their lesson from the cross: From dying to self comes life, from the ashes of fire come new opportunities for missional ministry. Reid says, "It was a 'bad blessing.'"[1]

9

Faith and Crisis

Experiencing God in the Eye of the Storm

Dr. William E. Hull–scholar, pastor, educator, and one of my mentors in ministry–wrote a benediction years ago that enfolds those receiving it in the all-encompassing presence of Christ:

Christ go before you,
to prepare a way of service;
Christ go behind you,
to gather up your efforts for his glory;
Christ go beside you,
as leader and guide;
Christ go within you,
as comfort and stay;
Christ go beneath you,
to uphold with everlasting arms;
Christ go above you,
to reign as Lord supreme.[1]

This exquisite blessing offers more than hope for the future; it offers faith-filled confidence in what already is. As the apostle Paul stated it in his speech to Athenians, "In him we live and move and have our being" (Acts 17:28).

Healthy congregations experience crisis with this sense of Christ's defining presence. It becomes their greatest asset during difficulty. Effective leaders center themselves and their congregations in this reality, putting God first, last, and at the center of all that occurs.

While none of the leaders with whom I spoke attributed their crises to God, they and their congregations opened themselves to lessons from God in the crises and saw God as intimately engaged in congregational response and recovery. They chose to engage their situations as opportunities for the development of faith and character, and as they journeyed through the crises, they experienced waves of gratitude for God's ongoing goodness.

Crisis heightened congregations' appreciation for their utter dependence on God. It drew them together in the fellowship of the Spirit. It drove them to their knees in prayer. It intensified their experiences of worship. It concentrated their attention on the insight and encouragement of scripture. It prompted spontaneous expressions of faith that they now preserve as part of their congregation's lore. It opened their eyes to evidence of God's loving, redemptive presence in the midst of their circumstances. It became a faith formative and transformative time in their lives.

These things didn't happen by accident. They happened at God's initiative, and congregational leaders played an essential role to facilitate their occurrence.

Facilitating a Congregation's Spirituality

Let's do a closer review of what this looks like in the life of congregations in crisis, drawing specific insights from leaders whose congregations have come out alive and well on the other side. What do their experiences suggest for facilitating the spirituality of a congregation in crisis?

Gather

A reverberating theme in conversations with crisis leaders is the theme of togetherness. Whether in times of corporate prayer and worship, informal get-togethers, or experiences of online community, the act of gathering is itself a spiritually potent act. As Jesus himself put it, "For where two or three are gathered in my name, I am there among them" (Matthew 18:20).

Never underestimate the power of human community in the context of crisis. As pastor and author John Ortberg observes, "In normal times, isolation hurts. In crisis, isolation kills. In normal times, community blesses. In crisis, community saves."[2]

Some people feel an instinctive impulse to rally together in times of crisis, while others have a tendency to withdraw. Leaders don't stand back and let nature take its course. They create opportunities to gather and leverage the potential of gatherings that are already on the congregation's calendar.

Formal Gatherings

Pastor Brady Boyd and his fellow leaders at New Life Church in Colorado Springs looked for the first opportunity to bring the congregation together after the deadly Sunday shooting. They scheduled a special gathering for Wednesday night and invited community leaders to join them. Boyd remembers with fondness how people poured into the "Living Room"–New Life's term for its worship space. They became "a sea of faith-filled people surrounding the public officials, police officers, fire fighters, and first responders" who had joined them for the occasion. A strength of corporate resolve came through in the congregational singing and prayers. Their hardiness could be heard in their vocal responses to the scriptures and preaching. The spirit of unity was palpable. That night became a defining moment for the congregation.

Small groups. New Lifers also experienced the spiritual power of community in their small group gatherings. On the occasion of Ted Haggard's resignation in disgrace and again after the shooting, these groups provided a holding environment of faith and mutual support. These clusters of friendship, Bible study, prayer, and service kept people from scattering when the center of leadership failed. They helped people heal when trauma might otherwise have overwhelmed them.

The body of Christ. Times of crisis present opportunities for experiencing and pointing to our oneness in Christ. When we act on our Spirit-infused instincts to rally together in tough times, we become living answers to the prayer Christ made on the night of his arrest: "And now I am no longer in the world, but they are in the world, and I am coming to you. Holy Father, protect them in your name that you have given me, so that they may be one, as we are one" (John 17:11). We are, said the apostle Paul, "The body of Christ" (1 Corinthians 12:27). "There is one body and one Spirit, just as you were called to the one hope of your calling, one Lord, one faith, one baptism, one God and Father of all, who is above all and through all and in all" (Ephesians 4:4–6).

When Sandy Run Baptist in Hampton, South Carolina, lost its historic sanctuary to a Sunday-morning fire, Pastor Paul Reid made sure the congregation remembered this. The body-of-Christ metaphor became a reverberating theme in their life together throughout the rebuilding process.

Social Media. Another way to enhance faith-filled fellowship is to leverage the spiritual potential of social media. We have already talked about the importance of the telephone and the Internet for crisis communications. Let's now affirm how, when constructively used, they become strands of love in the spiritually potent World Wide Web.

In the aftermath of First Baptist of Shreveport's bus accident, people used phone calls, texting, e-mail, cards, letters, and Facebook to extend their love and prayers. These served as means of our support for one another within the church. They also connected us to Christians around the world who reached out to us with empathy and goodwill. We enjoyed one of the most extraordinary benefits of new technology: its capacity to create a community unhindered by time zones and physical distance. We knew that we were being encompassed by prayer night and day. We received words of encouragement from people in other places who had been through crises themselves. We interacted with each other in ways that reinforced biblical faith and promoted our resiliency. We experienced ourselves as part of the worldwide body of Christ.

While affirming the potential of social media for promoting healing community in the midst of crisis, let's not pretend that it is a purely benign instrument of relationship. Social media can be used to undermine as well as build up the body. Furthermore, instantaneous communication has a viral quality about it, which means that questionable theology can spread just as rapidly as healthy theology.

A few days after First Baptist of Shreveport's bus accident, one of the youth who had been in the accident posted a picture on her Facebook wall of a bottle cap that she had found on her bathroom counter upon her return from the ill-fated trip. It had a message printed on the underside: "Miss the bus on purpose." Given recent circumstances, some of those who responded to the posting wondered if the bottle cap had been an overlooked warning. I felt obliged to introduce another perspective into the conversation, steering people away from fatalism and reminding them of the innocent meaning of the quote. The quote was simply encouraging us to season our sometimes overly planned, overly serious lives with playfulness and spontaneity.

Wise leaders keep themselves in the middle of social media not only to enjoy its benefits but also to influence its uses. They take initiative to affect the role it plays in shaping the congregation's experience.

God's presence and power flows into the life of the church gathered.

Worship

The foundational expression of the church gathered is corporate worship, and not surprisingly, crisis leaders consistently mention it first when recounting the spiritual dimension of their congregation's response to crisis. When we worship, we channel our shared stress in the direction of God. We enthrone God as Lord of our lives and as Master over the circumstances that have befallen us. We get drawn into the comfort of God's goodness and grace. We express our pain and call on God's mercy. We find our way into a holy space within which we can hear God's Word and respond in trust and commitment. Worship places us in the eye of the storm, where stillness, sanity, and perspective can overcome the chaos that crisis creates.

Worship at special times. Recognizing the essential role of worship in crisis response and recovery, congregational leaders give special attention to planning and preparation during seasons of stress. Especially valuable are these key worship experiences:

- *The first gathering of the congregation after the onset of crisis.* This may or may not occur at regularly scheduled weekend services. New Life's first gathering after the shooting took place on Wednesday night. University Baptist of Waco came together in a sister congregation's sanctuary on Sunday night, only hours after Kyle Lake's death. First Baptist Shreveport got news of the bus accident only moments before morning worship, but our first opportunity to gather after realizing the seriousness of the crisis came later the same afternoon at an already-scheduled "Songs We Love to Sing" worship experience.
- *The first Sunday after the crisis (if different from the first gathering).* Even though First Baptist had gathered multiple times during the first week after the bus accident, our Sunday morning worship service on July 19 held special meaning. Though we typically worshiped simultaneously in two separate venues, we held a joint service that morning and devoted careful attention to worship tone and flow, music, message, and the involvement of people who had been involved in the crisis and crisis response. Because of media interest, we also planned with a larger audience in mind.
- *Funerals and memorial services, if the crisis involved loss of life.* These become particularly important moments for expressing our grief, celebrating life, addressing faith issues, and resting our hope in God. Media interest adds an additional component to planning for these events, which demands that we plan with sensitivity to the needs of grieving family while also paying attention to our witness beyond the church as the people of God.
- *Pivotal points in the response and recovery process.* Sandy Run Baptist's groundbreaking service after its sanctuary fire was a pivotal moment, as were the dedications of memorial sites on the campuses of Wedgwood Baptist and New Life. On a Sunday morning one month after the bus accident, First Baptist Shreveport honored members of a National Guard unit that had played a heroic role at the crash scene. Any number of developments, whether they represent progress or setbacks, call for special awareness in worship preparation.
- *The first anniversary after the onset of crisis.* Some crises have fully resolved themselves before the first anniversary rolls around while many others have not. Either way, the first anniversary becomes a notable milestone, offering a natural opportunity to engage in a kind of holy remembering that encourages healing and hope. Virtually every congregation I studied did something special to note the occasion. Some incorporated their recognition into regular weekend worship services. Others held special events and included in the program those most significantly connected to the crisis. New Life, for instance, marked the first anniversary of the shooting with a candlelight vigil to which the public was invited. Family of lost loved ones played a special role in the service.

• *Holidays and other special occasions.* Major holidays in the year following congregational trauma can be especially difficult for those experiencing crisis-related grief. Worship planning, by keeping this in mind, can facilitate emotional and spiritual healing. There may be other circumstances unique to your context that afford special opportunities for a worship service that heals and renews. For instance, congregations that have experienced serious conflict will sometimes schedule services of reconciliation to mend relational fences in the presence of God.

Preparing for Worship at Special Times

Given the importance of worship to a congregation's crisis response and recovery, it's not surprising to hear congregational leaders talk about the special care with which they prepared for worship during the crisis. In preparations for our worship experience one week following the bus accident, First Baptist Shreveport's minister of music, Randy LeBlanc, and I had multiple conversations. He brought his own prayerful creativity to the planning process and consulted by phone and e-mail with friends in music ministry. I, too, thought long and hard about the moment. As a window into that planning process, what follows is an excerpt of a Tuesday-morning e-mail I sent to Randy:

> In terms of our focal interests as a church, Sunday morning's combined worship service must fulfill these high objectives:
>
> 1. It must be a sturdy declaration of Christian faith.
> 2. It must truly harmonize (not just represent) our worshiping communities.
> 3. Those involved in the accident must be represented.
> 4. The service must allow for "the voice of the people," which means that we may want other testimonials in addition to those of survivors, and we may also want to involve members as facilitators of a time of prayer.
> 5. Given the power of last Sunday night's hymn sing, we would do well to reprise elements from that.
> 6. We don't know what will be happening in the lives of those currently in the hospital and how this will impact the mood of the day, so the service must balance sobriety and celebration, concern and confidence.
> 7. My message will be something other than what I originally planned, and it will bring faith perspective to the moment.
> 8. If ever there were reason that the service might go longer than sixty minutes, this is the week. Achieving our worship aspirations will be more important than staying within narrow time parameters. My initial thought is that the service could be up to ninety minutes in length (and we will plan with this in mind, while

preparing ourselves for a serendipity of the Spirit).

These are beginning ideas. I will be interested in your perspective . . .

Let the Bible Speak

The Bible has an essential place in the life of the church at all times. In crisis, we turn to it with added intensity, hungry for hope and waiting for wisdom that we can apply to our urgent need. Our congregations don't just want to know what wise people have to say; they want to know what God has to say. The Bible provides this transcendent perspective. It speaks plainly about life and suffering in a fractured world.[3] It reminds us of God's compassion and crisis-conquering power.[4] It sustains us through trouble, with encouragement about where the journey will lead if we hold fast with trust in God.[5] It gives us permission to grieve, while keeping us anchored in hope.[6] It calls us to the way of Jesus, even when that way defies our natural impulses.

For example, Jesus' own behavior (Luke 23:34) and his instructions to "Love your enemies" (Matthew 5:44) and "Forgive others their trespasses" (Matthew 6:14–15) spoke directly to the people of Wedgwood Baptist after the eruption of violence in their church. It led them to pray for the capacity to respond as Jesus did and find the grace to forgive as he forgave.

I might also add that two particular texts of scripture stand out as texts to which the congregations in this study turned more often than any others in the midst of their crises:

- "In the world you face persecution. But take courage; I have conquered the world!" (John 16:33).
- "We know that in all things God works for the good of those who love God, who are called according to his purpose" (Romans 8:28, author's translation).

These foundational words of hope steadied these congregations as they reeled from the blows of crisis and found their footing again.

The Bible gives us not only words to *hear* but also words to *say* and *shout* and *sing.* We turn to the scriptures for the language of worship and find there words and moods for every occasion.

The Bible gave our congregation words to declare in defiance of our circumstances: "For I know whom I have believed and am persuaded that he is able to keep that which I've committed unto him against that day."[7] It provided psalms of lament to capture our hurt and our hope:

As the deer longs for flowing streams,
so my soul longs for you, O God.
My soul thirsts for God,

for the living God.
When shall I come and behold
the face of God?
(Psalm 42:1–2)

I remember, too, how moving it was when we concluded a time of corporate prayer by reciting together the Lord's Prayer:

Our Father in heaven,
hallowed be your name name . . .
(Matthew 6:9–13)

Scripture anchors a congregation's experience in the timeless wisdom and encouragement of God. We can saturate the environment with it through scripture readings and biblically centered litanies, prayers, and songs.

Interpret the Moment

It's not enough simply to let the Bible speak. As interpreters of scripture, we apply the Bible to our circumstances and suggest the ways it speaks to the moment.

Crises create anxiety and doubt. They unsteady our convictions. They raise uncomfortable questions: Why did this crisis happen? Where is God? Is it OK to grieve? Can we recover? How will we ever forgive? People turn to us with questions like these, and we play an instrumental role with our responses. From the pulpit, with the pen, in personal conversations, and by letting our lives speak, we influence how people deal with the unsettling faith questions raised by trauma.

Stubborn Confession

One of our roles in response to anxiety and doubt is to lead the congregation in a declaration of confidence in God. We claim God's promises and look to the future with hope. Chris Thacker, my friend in ministry and pastor of Emmanuel Baptist Church, Alexandria, Louisiana, has coined a phrase for this kind of declaration of faith. He calls it our stubborn confession.

Stubborn confession has a Timex quality to it. As the old watch commercials used to say, "It takes a licking and keeps on ticking." The prophet Habakkuk exemplified this kind of faith when he wrote,

Though the fig tree does not blossom,
and no fruit is on the vines;
though the produce of the olive fails
and the fields yield no food;
though the flock is cut off from the fold

and there is no herd in the stalls,
yet I will rejoice in the Lord;
I will exult in the God of my salvation.
(Habakkuk 3:17–18)

Much of our use of scripture in the midst of crisis has this purpose in mind. It's why Pastor Bill Klossner of Congregational United Church of Christ in Punta Gorda, Florida, pointed his congregation to Romans 8:28 on Sunday following Hurricane Charley, putting the Pauline promise in his own words: "Good things can come out of crisis." The congregation's ability to live into this conviction allowed them to recover rapidly and move on.

Permission to Grieve

Some people have difficulty experiencing and expressing emotion. Some Christians actually see tears as a sign of weakness. This can be a real problem when crisis erupts. Crisis inevitably brings loss, and loss brings grief. We grieve the loss of people, places, and things. We grieve irreversible changes to our way of life. Crisis brings grief, and grief brings tears.

Even though most of those we lead know these things in principle, it helps for us to remind them (and ourselves) that our grief is not a character flaw. It helps for us to sound the Bible's permission to mourn. Consider what Paul wrote to anxious Christians in Thessalonica. "We do not want you to be uninformed, brothers and sisters, about those who have died, so that you may not grieve as others do who have no hope" (1 Thessalonians 4:13). Paul understood that grieving was inevitable and healthy. He simply wanted them to hold onto their hope as they grieved.

This matters not only at a personal level but at a congregational level. For some reason, even in settings where individual grieving is understood and affirmed, the issue of a congregation's grieving isn't. Too many congregations try to move past the losses of crisis before they have fully recovered. The result is that many of the most serious, chronic problems congregations wrestle with can be traced back to unresolved emotions from crises in the past. When a congregation acts more like a secular institution than the body of Christ, the tendency is for outer signs of the wound to heal while an inner wound remains.

One of Pastor Brady Boyd's distinctive contributions to the healing of New Life Church after not one, but two traumatic developments in thirteen months, was to take the congregation's grief out of hiding and encourage openness about their pain. "We had two gaping wounds," he said, reflecting on what he saw in the life of the congregation. Through preaching, writing, and pastoral care, he reasserted the value of healthy grieving, giving individuals *and* the congregation time to heal from the inside out.

Constructive Theology

Congregations in crisis need theologically mature teaching and preaching. Sometimes this means counteracting misunderstandings and poor theology.

Take, for instance, the health and wealth gospel with its oversimplified guarantees of prosperity and happiness for faithful people. Those who buy into the notion that their goodness and faith will protect them against adversity set themselves up to feel devastated when troubles come. Related to this, consider what flows from the notion that catastrophe always has to do with God's punishment for sin.

When New Orleans fell into chaos after Hurricane Katrina, some very prominent Christians suggested in the press that the violence, death, and destruction represented God's retribution for the evils of the culture. Thankfully, other Christian leaders responded quickly to disavow such a notion. They spoke of God's compassion for those who were suffering and God's power to restore.

Catastrophology

As noted in the featured story on Wedgwood Baptist Church (at the outset of part 2), Pastor Al Meredith coined the term catastrophology to describe a theological perspective that accounts for evil and suffering. New Life pastor Brady Boyd echoed Meredith's perspective, criticizing what he called the "Fifth Gospel" preaching that removes suffering from its theology.

> We talk about this at New Life. We don't pursue suffering; but we know it's not *if,* but *when* suffering will come. We're caught between the cross and heaven. There is an "already" and "not yet" quality about our experience of Christ's kingdom.

In my message to family and friends at the funeral of Maggie Lee Henson, one of the two youth who died from bus-accident injuries, I spoke to this issue as well, offering a more helpful perspective about God's involvement in crisis:

> God is not the author of our tragedies. God is not some crafty conspirator who sets booby traps and orchestrates our disasters. God is not, in other words, a malicious, mischievous god who delights in our doom.
>
> Other forces, forces God permits—yes permits—but does not propel, get the blame for the blows that beat at us:
>
> - The dark conspiracy of spiritual powers and principalities
> - At times, the willful or witless behavior of evil or ignorant people—sometimes we ourselves are our worst enemies
> - The untamed forces of an unfinished creation (we live in a world

in which winds batter boats and tires blow and buses roll and mothers and fathers and brothers weep)

These are the culprits, not God. These are the agents of our undoing to which God, with God's greater power and goodwill responds.

God is not the author of all that befall us, but God *is* the author and finisher of our faith, the Benevolent Power who gets the last word. In Jesus' final conversation with disciples before his arrest and crucifixion he said, "In this world you shall have tribulation; but be of good cheer. I have overcome the world" (John 16:33, author's translation).

And where do we find God in the valley of the shadow of death, in the darkest hours, days, and seasons? As Psalm 23 tells us, we find God right at our side to guide and comfort and see us safely through to the other side (Psalm 23:4).

In fact, that is God's quiet answer to every "Why?" ever uttered in the face of suffering and death. "Why?" we cry, waiting for an answer. What God gives us is not a mindless stream of explanations, mere Band-Aids of benediction over the lacerations of our life. No, what God gives us as we cry, waiting for a word, is *the Word* –the Word made flesh. God gives us Jesus. He comes himself as Suffering Servant, to stand alongside us, not just as a historical comfort but as living Paraclete (that, after all, is the name Jesus gave to his ongoing presence, the Holy Spirit, the Paraclete, "the one who stands alongside to help.")

And more than that, he comes into the vortex of our grief and woe and takes our suffering into himself. His ultimate answer to our anguish and our anger is the cross. Jesus, on our behalf, allows himself to get sucked into the black hole of death. He gives into its light-extinguishing gravitational pull. He disappears into its abyss–that's the cross–and then comes out the other side–that's the resurrection–declaring, "Death has been swallowed up in victory!" (1 Corinthians 15:54, exclamation added).

That's God's answer. That's our consolation. God gives us Jesus. Brother and first born of all who are resurrected in him to life beyond death.

Sacred Silence

There are ways congregational leaders need to speak into the stress of crisis. There are also ways we need to fall silent. Crises take us to the edges of what we know about nature, people, organizations, and God. We need not pretend to know more than we know. In fact, we can help the people whose lives we steward by reminding them of the apostle Paul's observation in 1 Corinthians: "For now we see in a mirror, dimly, but then we will see face to face. Now I know only in part; then I will know fully, even as I have been fully known" (1 Corinthians 13:12). In fact, when all is said and done, *what we know* matters a lot less than that *we are fully known.* Helping our people relax into this in faith-filled trust will alleviate the unnecessary suffering that comes from our desire to control life and have an answer to every question.

I had this very thing in mind when, moments after hearing of the bus accident, I stepped to the platform as a leader of worship. When it came time to preach, I set aside the message I had prepared and turned to Philippians 4:6–7 instead, elaborating on it as an invitation for us all to turn anxiety toward prayer, while resting in the peace of God.

I also had this in mind when I spoke at the funeral three weeks later and said,

> Let's resist the temptation to say more than we can. Let's resist the temptation to strip this moment of its mystery out of an anxious need for easy answers. Let's live the lesson of Job's friends: that they were at their best in their silent companionship, before they opened their mouths. (Job 2:11–13)

In crises, God doesn't give us bumper-sticker bromides (easy answers and question-evading certitudes), but God does line the margins between time and eternity with declarations of reassurance and hope. Leaders help their congregations navigate life and faith along these margins.

The Power of Music

Saint Francis of Assisi once commented, "Preach the Gospel at all times, and when necessary use words." He said this knowing that actions speak louder than words. He could just as well have said this with music in mind. Music takes us to places words never can, and in times of crisis it has a unique power to hearten a congregation.

Among the music our congregation turned to for the Sunday following the bus accident was "Canticle of Hope,"[8] a moving choral piece composed by Joseph M. Martin (with lyrics by J. Paul Williams). "Canticle of Hope" was first dedicated to the people of Oklahoma City as they struggled to heal after the bombing of the Alfred P. Murrah Building on April 19, 1995. It begins quietly, affirming God as "perfect in holiness . . . the God of the needy and the poor . . . our sure defender . . . our refuge . . . the God who restores." Almost like a lullaby, the music conveys its message with tender understanding and gentle confidence. It swells briefly in the second half, declaring to God, "You are eternal. Alpha, Omega. We place our hope in you alone." Then it settles back into a quiet declaration of faith, ending with a melodic allusion to a classic hymn of assurance: "Great is Thy Faithfulness. Great is Thy Faithfulness. Great is Thy Faithfulness! You are the God who restores."

For a congregation in distress, an anthem like this one feels like being cradled in a mother's arms. It gives tears permission to flow. It soothes the soul. It settles the hurting heart securely in the strength and reliability of God. It does what words alone could never do by reaching beyond our emotional defenses to touch the inner places of our pain with the Spirit's healing grace.

Music at its best does just that, so it's not surprising that the stories of congregations' recovery from crisis include the soundtracks that accompanied them along the way. Whatever form they took, whether hymns of faith or contemporary worship songs, choral anthems or instrumentals, this music gave unforgettable, life-renewing encouragement to congregations in crisis.

You will want to take full advantage of the healing and confidence-building power of music. Hymns like "A Mighty Fortress Is Our God" and "It Is Well with My Soul" will provide your congregation words and tunes to lift the spirit. Contemporary songs like "For These Reasons" and "How Great Is Our God" will turn them toward God in faith-filled praise. In uncertain times, songs like "Be Still, My Soul" and "Trust His Heart" will steady you in the promises of God. Whether your congregation leans toward hymns, gospel songs, choruses, or scripture songs, you can match the music to the moment with great effect.

Your congregation may even have gifted musicians who can compose or arrange music to serve the congregation. Ross Parsley, New Life's worship minister at the time of Ted Haggard's resignation and subsequently the church's interim pastor, points to a song created for worship at New Life as a source of particular influence. "My Savior Lives," recorded and released in 2006,

> became a sound track for our experience. We're a strong worshiping community. It's part of the culture. Songs like this one gave us a way to fix our eyes on Jesus rather than on Ted or any other human leader.

Also take full advantage of instrumental music. Gifted keyboardists, guitarists, bell choirs, orchestras, and instrumental ensembles can speak deeply to the heart without ever uttering a word. I will never forget, for instance, the simple power of a guitarist and cellist performing Chris Tomlin's "Mighty Is the Power of the Cross"[9] during one of First Baptist Shreveport's postaccident worship services. The cello, with its almost-human voice, resonated with our longing for God's love, and the guitar captured our faith-filled confidence. You could have heard a pin drop as the last note lingered in the air.

Surrounding Your Circumstances in Prayer

Prayer threads its way through everything the congregation does in response to crisis. Whether it's a woman jumping to her feet while medical professionals tend to University Baptist of Waco's stricken pastor and shouting, "Let's pray!" or Hampton, South Carolina's Sandy Run Baptist dedicating its new sanctuary with expressions of thanks to God, a congregation breathes in and breathes out through prayer.

Prayer punctuates the turning points of crisis, concentrating our attention on God. It captures the spirit of each moment, whether in longing or gratitude. It involves listening as well as speaking, reminding us that what God has to say matters more than what we have to say. Corporate prayer is our congregation's ongoing conversation with the living God, whose presence and action in the midst of our circumstances spell the difference between defeat and renewal.

Calls to Prayer

Congregational leaders call their congregations to prayer, as the leaders of Holmeswood Baptist Church, Kansas City, Missouri did when financial issues put us on high alert. We decided to treat our financial crisis as a time of renewal and incorporated a twenty-four-hour prayer vigil into our plans. One fourth of the adult membership participated, many of them coming to the church in the still of the night to pray on behalf of the congregation.

Spontaneous Prayer

Some of a congregation's praying happens at the initiative of its official leaders, but not all of it. In fact, some of the most powerful praying in times of crisis comes unbidden. In a permission-giving congregational culture, members can be counted on to take their own initiative to pray.

As I have already mentioned, First Baptist of Shreveport went ahead with its plans for a hymn sing on the evening of the bus accident. Not surprisingly, attendance far exceeded what we had anticipated when planning the event. Though we altered the program to make time for an update and an extended time of prayer, the impulse for prayer overflowed beyond the service.

During my update to the congregation, a member asked, "Is it possible for those who are interested to stay after the service for a time of prayer in the parlor?" My answer, of course, was, "By all means!" A crowd of people filled the parlor and lingered for more than an hour to pray.

The next day, two young women in the church came by asking for permission to rally members again that evening for prayer in the church chapel. They didn't need someone from the ministerial staff to organize and lead the congregation's prayer response.

Prayers for All Seasons

Our praying doesn't just happen at the low points of crisis. It plays an integral role at every point along the way, from onset to resolution. For this reason, our praying ranges from anguished lament to celebration and praise. One of our high privileges and responsibilities as prayer leaders is to capture the nature of the moment and facilitate the prayers of the people accordingly.

Depending on the faith tradition within which you operate, you may or may not be in the practice of using pre-formed prayers. It certainly deserves a place of special consideration for those with prayer leadership responsibilities. Giving thought in advance of corporate times of prayer adds mindfulness, range, and depth to yours and the congregation's praying. Furthermore, we can all benefit from streams of Christian faith other than our own, whose records of prayer can enrich the way we enter into the presence of God. I, for instance, have benefitted greatly by turning to *The Book of Common Prayer* in preparation for special times of corporate prayer.

Answered Prayers

Many of us can identify with the nine lepers, who experienced Jesus' healing and didn't think to return and give thanks (Luke 17:11–19). It's more natural to ask for things than to say thank you. Congregationally speaking, it's more common for us to pray in our distress than it is for us to notice God's answers.

We experienced an early reminder of God's grace at First Baptist of Shreveport. Forty-seven citizen soldiers of the 2101 Transport Company of the Alabama National Guard were on a chartered bus directly behind ours when the accident happened. On their way home from weekend maneuvers, having that very weekend trained for up-righting overturned vehicles and handling medical emergencies on the battlefield, they were perfectly situated and freshly trained. They handled things with skill and tenderness, saved lives, and brought comfort to our traumatized loved ones. We had many opportunities to thank them in the weeks that followed. When we did, we repeated what became a refrain of prayerful thanks: "Though you didn't know it at the time, you were traveling east on I-20 that morning on a divine appointment."

Everything good that emerges from our crises and every sign of progress and recovery becomes an occasion to celebrate God's goodness. It becomes part of the healing cycle by which God is honored and our morale returns.

Knowing When to Direct the Action and When to Get Out of the Way

How good are you at balancing initiative and permission giving? Do you tend to err on the side of letting things happen or on the side of controlling every detail? As a spiritual leader during crisis, it's important for you to exercise your influence on the faith development of your congregation. It's also important for you to support and enjoy the spiritual initiative and resiliency of your people. Given half an opportunity, many will step forward in amazing ways, and you will have expressions of congregational health on which to draw (and toward which to point!) for years to come.

At New Horizon Christian Church, Pastor Jim Bane didn't have to ask before skilled members were volunteering their time and expertise to repair and remodel the water-damaged church facility. "People stepped up," Bane says, "and it invigorated the volunteer spirit of the congregation."

When the founding pastor of New Journey Church in Olathe, Kansas, felt led to leave the church for ministry in another part of the state, the young congregation faced uncertainty about its ability to survive, let alone thrive. Some members left. Giving dropped. But those who remained renewed their commitment to God's vision for their church. "We had let the pastor carry too much of the load," they now say. His departure drew out their best. They are smaller in number now, but more resilient and missional. Eighty percent of their members recently participated in a serving opportunity in the city.

Christ is present in our crises, surrounding us and filling us and guiding us every step of the way. Through Christ, we have resources at our disposal that secular organizations can only envy. As we put them into play, we experience the power of God that prevails over adversity.

Reflection Questions

Reflect personally on the following questions. If you are using this book with a study group, share your perspectives with each other. If you aren't currently experiencing a congregational crisis, think of a crisis your congregation has experienced or might experience and project yourself into that situation when reflecting on the questions.

- What are *your* congregation's greatest faith assets for surviving and even thriving through crisis?
- What potential faith assets could you bring into play more intentionally?
- What evidence of God have you seen as your congregation moves through crisis?
- What are you doing to promote congregational awareness and gratitude as it relates to God's presence and action?

10

Going the Distance

Leading through Crisis without Burning Out

The 2011 U.S. Open, held at Congressional Country Club in Bethesda, Maryland, provided historic theater thanks to Rory McIlroy. A gifted twenty-two-year-old golfer from Northern Ireland, McIlroy arrived at the year's second major tournament with the word "choke" hovering over him because of his performance in the first. Two and a half months earlier, he had stood at the first tee on the final day of the Masters with a seemingly insurmountable four-stroke lead, only to have his game fall apart under the pressure. In a round that included a triple bogey, he shot an eight-over-par 80 and finished ten strokes behind the tournament champion.

At the U.S. Open, seemingly undaunted by his earlier collapse, McIlroy dominated the rest of the field, leading by three after the first round, six after the second round, and eight going into the final eighteen holes on Sunday. As he stepped up to the first tee, the question on everybody's mind was whether he would repeat his Masters collapse or keep his cool and prevail. He answered the question resoundingly, closing out the tournament with a two-under-par 69 to claim an eight-stroke win and the champion's trophy. His final score of 268 (sixteen under par) shattered the old tournament record by four strokes. He had slain the psychological dragon and led from start to finish, showing tremendous poise under pressure.

In the game of golf they talk about course management—thinking and playing your way around a golf course to avoid hazards and maximize opportunities. Those who do this well make a very good living at the sport.

As Rory McIlroy's story demonstrates, there's yet another aspect of the game that's equally, if not more, important. It's called *self*-management. The ability to manage oneself while managing the course spells the difference between victory and defeat—especially if it means making a comeback after humiliating loss.

It doesn't take a great leap of the imagination to see how this translates into leading through crisis. As crisis leaders, we pick ourselves up after misfortune, confront hazards and opportunities, and work our way through them in a collaborative partnership with God and others. We know that our self-management matters as much, if not more, than our management of the circumstances and our leadership of people.

Resilience

Crisis leadership provides a severe test of poise under pressure. It forces us to deal with setbacks and disarray, knowing all the while that others are looking to us for reassurance and direction. It calls for decisiveness and flexibility under time constraints and uncertain conditions. It challenges our durability and presents us with problems that can't be fixed overnight.

Crisis leadership, in other words, calls for resilience. The American Psychological Association (APA) defines resilience as "the process of adapting well in the face of adversity, trauma, tragedy, threats, or even significant sources of stress . . . It means 'bouncing back' from difficult experiences."[1]

Jerry Patterson, professor of leadership studies at the University of Alabama at Birmingham and a leading authority on the topic of leadership resilience, has identified three broad skill sets that distinguish resilient leaders:

- *Thinking skills*. Resilient leaders show what Patterson calls "realistic optimism." They have the ability to face the facts, the good news and the bad. At the same time, they remain confident that good can come from the adverse circumstances confronting them.
- *Capacity skills*. Resilient leaders are fueled by their personal values, their confidence and competence, their physical-emotional-spiritual wellbeing, and their network of care and support. The stronger and fresher these are, the better able leaders are to weather turbulent times.
- *Action skills*. Resilient leaders take prompt, sustained, and principled action during difficult situations. They persevere, refusing to let adversity prevail. They adapt by remaining flexible and creative to solve problems. They show courage by acting with decisiveness in the face of ambiguity and uncertainty. They accept personal responsibility for mistakes and solutions.[2]

How do these skills come into play in the life of a congregational leader? What can we do to cultivate them in the crunch?

Thinking Skills: Cultivating the Spirit of Realistic Optimism

Those of us who lead through congregational crisis show resilience, first of all, by anchoring our service in faith-filled hope. Refusing to dodge the facts, we press into the challenges with our eyes wide open. At the same time, we maintain confidence that we and the church have what it takes to prevail.

The interesting thing about this confidence in the life of a spiritually centered leader is that it's more about *God*-confidence than *self*-confidence. That's precisely the kind of realistic confidence that Jesus promotes in John: "In the world you face persecution. But take courage; I have conquered the world!" (John 16:33). Across time, God's kind of leaders have remained grounded in reality and anchored in faith.

Consider the Old Testament story of Joseph (Genesis 37–50). Betrayed by his brothers, Joseph gets taken in slavery to Egypt. Facing up to his circumstances, he distinguishes himself in service and rises to a position of trust in his master's household. Seduced by his master's wife, he refuses to compromise his values, landing himself in prison with his integrity intact. There he distinguishes himself again, gaining influence behind bars. Years later, when the opportunity presents itself, he is ready to act, interpreting the pharaoh's dream and earning himself a position as chief operating officer of the entire empire.

Joseph's faith-filled resilience shines through in his ability to adapt to adversity and thrive. It also rings loudly and clearly in his later interpretation of the course of his life. A severe drought brings his family to Egypt, and he tends to their need, despite his brothers' earlier betrayal. When his father dies, his brothers understandably fear for their lives, but Joseph puts them at ease: "Don't be afraid! Even though you intended to do harm to me, God intended it for good, in order to preserve a numerous people, as he is doing today" (Genesis 50:19–20). That's God-grounded, hope-filled, field-tested resilience.

How can we promote in our mind and heart this kind of realistic optimism? A good starting point is *rehearsing the promises of God*. In the midst of crisis, while we're inspiring hope in others, we can soak up the same inspiration for ourselves by looking to the scriptures and our own experiences to reinforce our convictions.

That's what I was doing on the Sunday morning of the bus accident when I decided on the spur of the moment to set aside my sermon notes and preach on Philippians 4:6–7. As I began, I told everyone, "I need to hear these words right now as much as anyone. In the uncertainty of this moment, let's take these words like prescription medication for our souls." Then I recited the verses and elaborated on them as a source of encouragement for us all:

> Don't worry about anything, but in everything by prayer and supplication with thanksgiving let your requests be made known to

God. And the peace of God, which surpasses all understanding, will guard your hearts and your minds in Christ Jesus. (Philippians 4:6–7)

Psalm 1 reminds us just how important it is for us to stay rooted in scripture, training our mind in keeping with its outlook on life. Those whose "Delight is in the law" and who "Meditate day and night" are

Like trees
planted by streams of water,
which yield their fruit in its season,
and their leaves do not wither.
In all that they do, they prosper
(Psalm 1:2–3)

We can apply the core wisdom of this Psalm to our situations. In times of crisis, it serves us well to *delight in* and *meditate on* selections of scripture that reinforce realistic hope.[3]

We also do well to rehearse our personal experiences of coming through past difficulties. In keeping with Hebrew tradition, which places a premium on *remembering*, we gain confidence by seeing our current prospects in the light of previous outcomes.

That's what the apostle Paul was doing when, locked away in prison, he drew strength from decades of experience with God's faithfulness:

Not that I am referring to being in need; for I have learned to be content with whatever I have. I know what it is to have little, and I know what it is to have plenty. In any and all circumstances I have learned the secret of being well-fed and of going hungry, of having plenty and of being in need. I can do all things through him who strengthens me. (Philippians 4:11–13)

Over time, as experience confirms what biblical faith teaches–as it confirms that good can come from the bad things that happen to us–we develop a deep reservoir of confidence for facing the challenges that come our way. Interestingly enough, the APA recommends this very thing. Their resource, "The Road to Resilience," suggests that we draw on personal history by asking the following questions:

• What kinds of events have been most stressful for me?
• How have those events typically affected me?
• Have I found it helpful to think of important people in my life when I am distressed?
• To whom have I reached out for support in working through a traumatic or stressful experience?

- What have I learned about myself and my interactions with others during difficult times?
- Has it been helpful for me to assist someone else going through a similar experience?
- Have I been able to overcome obstacles, and if so, how?
- What has helped make me feel more hopeful about the future?[4]

When combined with faith-reinforcing exercises, questions like these help anchor us in realistic hope. They put us back in touch with our resourcefulness and remind us that we have good reason to think positively about our future prospects and those of the church.

We can cultivate a spirit of realistic optimism.

Capacity Skills: Calling on Personal and Relational Reserves

We can also cultivate our internal and interpersonal capacities. In fact, this lies at the heart of resilient leadership. According to Jerry Patterson, "resilience capacity" is something like "the fuel tank that supplies necessary energy to produce resilient actions."[5] To sustain ourselves as we engage the challenges of crisis, we draw on our personal values, our sense of confidence and competence, and our relationships with God and others. Expanding these reserves and keeping them replenished is crucial.

No surprises there, right? We know that we must continuously check our bearings against the internal compass of our personal values. We know that we are fueled by living consistently with those values. We know that we must tend to our physical, mental, and relational health. We know that the condition of our relationship with God will inform all these areas.

There's a term for what happens when we neglect these things. It's called *burnout*.

Burnout

Burnout is a serious issue among clergy in general. According to an August 1, 2010, *New York Times* article,

> Members of the clergy now suffer from obesity, hypertension and depression at rates higher than most Americans. In the last decade, their use of antidepressants has risen, while their life expectancy has fallen. Many would change jobs if they could.[6]

A 2009 study conducted by Fuller Institute, George Barna, and Pastoral Care, Inc. found the following:

- 90 percent of the pastors report working between 55 and 75 hours per week.
- 80 percent believe pastoral ministry has negatively affected their families.

- 75 percent report that they have experienced a significant stress-related crisis at least once in their ministry.
- 90 percent feel they are inadequately trained to cope with their ministry demands.
- 50 percent feel unable to meet the demands of the job.
- 70 percent say they have a lower self-image now than when they first started.
- 70 percent do not have someone they consider a close friend.
- 50 percent have considered leaving the ministry in the last month.[7]

These statistics come from the general population of ministers. Imagine what these statistics would look like if the study focused on those leading their congregations through crisis! Crisis leadership makes heavier than normal demands on our fuel sources. It heightens our risk of running on empty.

Lies We Tell Ourselves

My wife Priscilla and I have different attitudes about refueling our cars. I like to wait until the low-fuel warning light goes on. She prefers to stop at a gas station before the gauge drops to one-quarter full. In my clearer moments, I know that her way makes more sense than mine, but at a gut level, stopping at the gas station feels like a detour. I want to keep going. I'm still hoping that someday they'll invent tanker trucks that can refuel cars while they're rolling.

It sounds crazy, doesn't it? We know that refueling is one of the rules of the road and that taking time for doing so is ultimately the only way to keep going. Why is it, then, that when it comes to running our lives, so many of us wait until our internal warning light starts blinking before we tend to our needs?

By way of explanation, consider three lies that seduce us. The first is *the myth of invincibility.* Distorting "I can do all things through Christ who gives me strength" (Philippians 4:13, author's translation) to mean that God gives us magical powers, we imagine ourselves immune to the normal rules of human finitude. Here's what author and conference speaker Ruth Haley Barton has to say:

> It is an embarrassing little secret, common among leaders, and we need to be more honest about it: buried deep in the psyche of many leaders is a Superman mentality—that somehow we are not like other human beings, and we can function beyond normal human limitations and save the world. Or at least our little corner of the world. This is a myth that we indulge to our peril.[8]

The second lie we buy into is *the myth of indispensability.* We tell ourselves that we *have* to keep going, that everyone's depending on us, that everything will fall apart if we step back—even for a day. Rae Jean Proeschold-Bell, an assistant professor of health research at Duke University and director of one of many studies on clergy burnout, says, "These people tend to be driven by a sense of a duty to God to answer every call for help from anybody, and they are virtually called upon all the time, 24/7."[9] She notes that one of those interviewed hadn't taken a vacation in eighteen years.

Psychologists have a name for this kind of behavior; it's called co-dependence, and they place it in the category of addictions. Unfortunately, it's one of those addictions many congregational cultures applaud, telling us to rest while patting us on the back for "always being there."[10]

The third lie that hooks us is *the myth of isolation.* We tell ourselves that we don't have time for friendships. We tell ourselves that nobody could possibly understand us. We convince ourselves that it's not safe to tell another human being what's really stirring around inside.

Were you startled by the statistic that 70 percent of the ministers surveyed said they didn't have someone they considered a close friend? Clearly, one of the ironies of congregational leadership is that we live in the public eye and carry on ministry neck-deep in relationships, but still struggle with loneliness. Many of us can relate to something Janis Joplin once said after a big concert: "I've just made love to 25,000 people, and I'm going home alone."[11]

If we're going to lead through crisis without burning out, we've got to shatter the myths of invincibility, indispensability, and isolation. We've got to accept our limits, include self-care in the rhythm of our lives, and look beyond ourselves as well as within ourselves for the fuel sources that energize us.

A Proactive Plan for Capacity Building

The best way to beat burnout is to prevent it in the first place. But even if you've let the tank go low, there are steps you can take to refuel.

We'll be talking about holistic spirituality here, by the way. Rather than seeing spiritual, physical, intellectual, emotional, and relational health as separate slices of a pie and confining God to one of them, let's affirm that every aspect of capacity building is a deeply spiritual act. Seeing things this way actually gives us a better appreciation for what it means to "Love the Lord your God with all your heart, and with all your soul, and with all your mind, and with all your strength" (Mark 12:30). We are loving God when we take each of these areas of our lives seriously.

Also note that stress management is an essential ingredient in each of these areas of capacity building. Unrelenting stress will wind us up and break us down physically, mentally, emotionally, and relationally. The high demands of crisis leadership call for balancing activity with rest, seriousness with playfulness, and sociality with solitude. Taking care of this balance is an essential element in what twelfth-century abbot Bernard of Clairvaux spoke of as "the love of self for God's sake."[12]

Carry on a Loving Relationship with God

My student ministry director at Baylor University, Lonnie Hayter, once told of a time when the stresses of his job had him on spiritual autopilot. Preparing to lead a contingent of two hundred students to Singapore-Malaysia for a spring break mission trip, he worked obsessively to put every detail in place. One afternoon, shortly before departure day, he was sitting at his office desk reviewing plans when an inward voice interrupted with a question. "Lonnie, do you love me?"

The question shook him, then drove him to his knees in tearful prayer. He realized that he had been so busy working for God that he hadn't taken time to enjoy God. Task had overtaken relationship as the focus of his faithfulness. "Yes, Lord," he answered. "I do love you. I love you with all my heart!"

If ever there's a time when task can overtake relationship as the focus of our faithfulness, it's when we're in crisis-response mode. So let's remind ourselves how much God loves us and how restless our hearts are until we find our rest in God.[13] Our joy and the sustainability of our leadership depend on staying plugged into God. The starting point and center point and final aim of life is relationship with God, and we know that we put ourselves in the best position to receive this grace through such disciplines as prayer, immersion in scripture, meditation, solitude, and worship.

What are you doing to feed your soul? Do you have a relationship with God apart from pragmatic preparations for preaching and teaching? Are you finding ways for "wasting time" with God?

Everything that follows in this section flows from life in community with God. Consider, then, these other areas for building your personal capacity.

Listen to Your Body and Treat It Kindly

Are you short on sleep? Are you overeating or undereating or trashing out on too much junk food? Have you neglected a common-sense program of exercise? I'll spare you the guilt-trip of talking about your body as "God's temple" (1 Corinthians 3:16–17)—you already know that God created you, resides in you, and cares about your bodily existence. I'll also spare you the details of getting these things right—there's no shortage of resources out there for developing healthy physical habits.

Let me simply remind you that your body is constantly talking to you—or, to put it another way, God is constantly talking to you through your body—and it pays to listen. Healthy eating fights off diseases, enhances sleep, and controls weight. Exercise reduces stress, improves mood, and boosts endurance. Sleep, recreation, and relaxation give your body a chance to recover from the demands that your life is placing on it.

Let's focus particularly on the need for rest in the rhythm of your life, especially in light of the ways crisis leadership can get this rhythm out of sync. The truth is that except for short bursts of circumstance when the real demands of crisis leadership trump your need for balance, *you*–not your situation–will dictate how much rest you get. Sandy Run pastor Paul Reid was smart. Despite the congregational challenges of rebuilding after the fire, he and his family kept their vacation plans. He took time to go fishing. He knew when to call it quits at the end of the day.

After an extended period of high stress, we almost certainly need more than the normal day-to-day and week-to-week breaks from work. A few weeks after the on-campus shooting, New Life's elders wisely insisted that Brady Boyd take a three-day rest-and-renewal break. "I was toast," admits Boyd. "Those three days were very redeeming. I knew I had a long journey ahead of me."

Tend to Unresolved Emotions

Best-selling author and pastor Gordon MacDonald tells of an experience early in his pastoral career when a combination of factors–conducting two funerals, extreme busyness, and internal unrest while reconsidering some of his longstanding beliefs–left him emotionally vulnerable. One Saturday morning at breakfast, his wife innocently said to him, "You haven't spent any time with the family this month." He burst into tears, a reaction that caught him completely off guard.

Here's what he has to say, looking back on that occasion:

> During this dark moment, I discovered that unresolved feelings do not flutter away in the wind. They deposit themselves in the strata of our souls and lie waiting to escape. They're all there: the resentments, the despair, the anxieties, the worries, the fears [*and I might add, the grief*].[14]

Pushing them underground only complicates things. MacDonald now keeps a record of his feelings, journaling each day to take inventory of the previous twenty-four hours. By his own admission, this isn't a fail-safe strategy, but it helps him stay current about his emotions and tend to them while they're fresh.

Are you taking seriously the emotional impact of crisis leadership? Do you have a strategy for tending to this dimension of your life? Perhaps prayerful journaling is the perfect solution for you. Perhaps you do best when you have the listening ear of a confidant. It may be that you need the professional support of a counselor to understand and process your emotions. The bottom line is this: Take healthy steps–every day and on an ongoing basis–to tend to your emotions.

Realign Yourself with Healthy Values

Much of our resilient capacity comes from a sense of integrity, the sense that we are living in alignment with a clearly defined set of core values. Yet even if we have defined for ourselves what these are and have cultivated them under normal circumstances, the conditions of crisis put a severe strain on them.

Ministry under pressure can turn us into short-sighted pragmatists. We can find ourselves making decisions based primarily on gut instincts; the pushes and pulls of strong-willed, high-anxiety people; and our own reactivity to unfolding developments. We can give in to inappropriate alternatives for nurturing ourselves. Crises also have a way of stripping away the veneer of our stated values and exposing the actual values that are driving us. If we hope to live in harmony with the best principles of a Spirit-centered life, we must revisit those principles regularly and realign ourselves with them.

This is another good reason for maintaining the habits of spiritual formation, whatever the external circumstances of our lives. The demands of crisis may tempt us to think we don't have time; but if anything, our need for these disciplines goes up, not down during challenging times. Martin Luther is well known for having extended his time in prayer when he experienced life putting added demands on him: "I have so much business I cannot get on without spending three hours daily in prayer."[15]

You don't have to measure yourself against Martin Luther's three-hour standard to know the essential wisdom of reserving time for prayerful realignment when life heats up. How are your habits of devotion? Do you set aside daily time for meditation, prayer, and study? Are you designating a place in your weekly calendar for solitude and personal reflection?

The first benefit of this, of course, is the joy of keeping undistracted company with God. But these habits serve to keep our lives centered too. They become the means by which we invite God to develop our character and keep us calibrated.

> Search me, O God, and know my heart;
> test me and know my thoughts.
> See if there is any wicked way in me,
> and lead me in the way everlasting.
> (Psalm 139:23–24)

Draw Strength from Relationships

Do you remember pastor and author John Ortberg's statement in the previous chapter? "In normal times, isolation hurts. In crisis, isolation kills. In normal times, community blesses. In crisis, community saves."[16] Supportive relationships can spell the difference between whether we thrive through crisis or give way under its weight.

Notice the qualifier. What we want to look for and cultivate are *supportive* relationships–relationships with people who lighten our loads and lift our spirits, relationships with people who stick by us unconditionally and who, because we give them permission, can speak the truth in love. The congregational leaders I know have more than their share of relationships; but they have a much smaller pool of relationships that qualify in one or more of these ways.

What are you doing to build trusting relationships with those who can support you in tough times? How readily do you acknowledge your weaknesses and limitations and turn to others who have strengths in those areas? Are you making healthy choices about who you get close to? Do you have confidants with whom you feel safe to share your doubts and fears, mentors or role models to whom you can turn for guidance, and friends with whom you can celebrate big and little victories? These relationships will sustain you.

The Lilly Endowment has brought particular attention to the importance of peer relationships for clergy resilience. In a recent review of outcomes from one set of Lilly-sponsored groups, professor and grant director John Mark Mulder observes, "There is a collective wisdom in groups of clergy sharing their hopes and fears and finding in each other the ways to nurture excellence. In other words, the 'wounded healers' can heal each other."[17]

I had actually been facilitating a clergy peer group for several years when the bus accident occurred. From personal experience, I can echo Mulder's perspective. My peer group buoyed my spirits when the stresses of crisis leadership weighed me down. These colleagues gave me a context of friendship within which to be transparent and regain perspective. If you're not in a peer group, I would encourage you to find one. If one doesn't exist, start one, even if it means just inviting a ministry friend or two to lunch and having an informal group around you. It matters that much.

Aim Yourself and Get Organized

In a study on clergy burnout conducted by Austin Presbyterian Theological Seminary in partnership with the Favrot Fund, 74 percent of pastors reported that their greatest stress comes from the struggle to determine priorities and organize their work. That makes perfect sense to me. Over the years of ministry, one of my chief sources of stress has been fuzzy thinking. When I lack clarity about the end toward which I'm aiming or the means by which I'll get there, a restless kind of distress replaces calm confidence. Fortunately, the flipside is also true. When I sort things out and get a game plan, my mood brightens.

Crisis creates a perfect recipe for fuzzy thinking. It overturns order and douses us in uncertainty. To get a leg up, we need to regain a sense of where we're heading and our means for getting there. This actually takes us back to the advice earlier in this book that we collaborate with other leaders in our congregation to develop goals and objectives for responding to and recovering from crisis. Here's the point: Not only will it help your congregation if you take these steps but it will also help you. It will bring purpose and clarity to your life and ministry. Doing it in partnership with others has the added benefit of reassuring you that there's leadership consensus about your priorities. You're liberated from enervating uncertainty about the expectations of others.

Action Skills: The Bounce-Back Effect of Facing and Solving Problems

Resilient leadership grows stronger as we cultivate our *thinking* and *capacity* skills. We can also cultivate *action* skills, the third of the skill sets Jerry Patterson discovered in his research on resilient leaders. This, actually, has been the focus this book. We have devoted our attention to what it looks like for leaders to act wisely, decisively, and compassionately over the course of crisis response and recovery. Patterson's research suggests that your action-oriented response to difficulty will itself enhance your resilience. You will experience a personal bounce-back effect from tackling the problems and leveraging the opportunities created by crisis.

In his phenomenal best seller, *The Road Less Traveled,* psychiatrist Scott Peck confronts the human tendency to bemoan difficulties and avoid problems. This tendency is understandable, given that confronting problems and solving them necessitates suffering. Unfortunately, when we avoid our problems we actually allow our problems *and* our suffering to worsen. Peck sees the capacity to confront and solve life's problems as a core component of mental health.[18]

George Bernard Shaw must have had something of this in mind when he wrote,

> This is the true joy in life, the being used for a purpose recognized by yourself as a mighty one; the being a force of nature instead of a feverish, selfish little clod of ailments and grievances complaining that the world will not devote itself to making you happy.[19]

Shaw understood that joy yields itself to those who throw themselves into life, with all its contingencies, rather than waiting for joy to fall into their laps.

There is actually something energizing about plugging into problems and doing something about them, an experience mentioned by virtually every congregational leader with whom I spoke. When, instead of feeling overwhelmed by our crises, we engage them and set about putting the broken pieces together again, we shift from the role of victim to active agent. As we see order restored and progress made, our confidence and hope grows. As people of faith, we have a conscious awareness that God has supplied the strength that enables our action and the benefits that grow out of our action (Philippians 2:12–13).

We have a record of the apostle Paul encouraging several churches in just this way. Here are two examples. To Christians in Corinth, he wrote,

"Therefore, my beloved, be steadfast, immovable, always excelling in the work of the Lord, because you know that in the Lord your labour is not in vain" (1 Corinthians 15:58). To Christians in Galatia, he added, "So let us not grow weary in doing what is right, for we will reap at harvest time, if we do not give up" (Galatians 6:9).

How often do you pause to reflect on the progress you and your congregation have made because of problems you've dealt with and opportunities you've claimed? Doing this will heighten your gratitude toward God. It will also heighten your joy and confidence as one who, with a high sense of purpose, is doing what needs to be done. Any leader, whether wired by God with a built-in bias for action or not, has stories to which they can turn.

The goal of this exercise, of course, isn't just to *feel* resilient, but to *be* resilient. The goal isn't just to imagine yourself as effective, but to sustain and grow your effectiveness.

When it comes to action, how are you doing? Are you experiencing the satisfaction of living fully into your situation, or are you stuck? Are there problems you've needed to confront or opportunities you've needed to seize that still await your initiative? If so, is it possible that the time has come to get on with it? The lesson of the action skill set is that you'll feel better if you do.

One time when I was buckling under the weight of stress in ministry, I turned to a trusted colleague as an outlet for my pain. It had gotten to the point at which I was struggling even to keep basic ministry going. The idea of *thriving* in ministry seemed totally beyond the realm of possibility; I just hoped to *survive!* My friend reassured me that he had been where I was—more than once. He then passed along some simple advice that someone else had given him to help him get over the hump: "Each day, think of one thing you can do that feels life affirming and productive, and then do it."

Trying out his idea gave me a renewed measure of control over my life. I had gotten so overwhelmed by the size of my challenges that I had become immobilized. This, in turn, hampered my work and lowered my self-esteem. It created a downward spiral of procrastination and discouragement, which wasn't good for me or those I led. Acting on my friend's advice, I gradually broke free from inertia. Even little steps were difficult at first, but the simple process of doing at least one life-affirming and productive thing each day reversed the downward spiral and created positive momentum.

This is resilience through action. To borrow a phrase from the Letter of James, God wants us to "Be doers of the word, and not merely hearers" (James 1:22). God wants us to feel the satisfaction of full participation in God's recreative work.

Going the Distance

Leadership through crisis isn't a sprint, though there may be occasions when sprinting is required. I'm not even sure that it's best to compare it to a long-distance run, despite biblical references of this nature and the fact that it requires endurance if we hope to finish well.[20] Sports metaphors can feel relentless and exhausting when what we're needing are metaphors that energize and encourage us. They can also feed competitive instincts that isolate us from our potential support system.

The Bible's best metaphor for crisis leadership may be the *journey*,[21] an image that opens up a wider set of possibilities. It aims us at a destination but gives meaning to everything that happens between here and there. It invites us to pace ourselves and explore the full potential of wherever we are at any point in time. It encourages us to take in the views along the way. It creates the possibility of companionship, which turns an otherwise lonely enterprise into a shared adventure. It reminds us that though we may not know exactly where we'll end up, God knows where we're going and escorts us every step of the way.

May God bless you and your congregation richly wherever your journey takes you.

> Now to him who is able to keep you from falling, and to make you stand without blemish in the presence of his glory with rejoicing, to the only God our Saviour, through Jesus Christ our Lord, be glory, majesty, power, and authority, before all time and now and for ever. Amen. (Jude 24–25)

Reflection Questions

Reflect personally on the following questions. If you are using this book with a study group, share your perspectives with each other. If you aren't currently experiencing a congregational crisis, think of a crisis your congregation has experienced or might experience and project yourself into that situation when reflecting on the questions.

- How would you rate yourself in terms of the thinking, capacity, and action skills of a resilient leader? What are your greatest strengths? What are your greatest vulnerabilities?
- What might you do to enhance your strengths and deal with your vulnerabilities? What one thing might you change that would most improve your resilience?
- To whom are you willing to make yourself accountable about your resilience-building commitments?

Notes

Chapter 1: One Minister's Tales of Crisis

[1] The mission of Directions, Inc., is to serve people as they lead their organizations, relationships, and lives. Providing consultation services to congregations is integral to our nonprofit mission. You can learn more about Directions, Inc., on my Web site, http://www.GregoryLHunt.com.

Chapter 2: Understanding Congregational Crisis

[1] M. Scott Peck, *The Road Less Traveled: A New Psychology of Love, Traditional Values and Spiritual Growth* (New York: Simon & Schuster, 1978), 15.

[2] Howard W. Stone, *Crisis Counseling* (Philadelphia: Fortress Press, 1976), 12–14.

[3] Raymond B. Flannery Jr. and George S. Everly Jr., "Crisis Intervention: A Review," *International Journal of Emergency Mental Health* 2(2) (2000): 119.

[4] Webster's Dictionary defines *crisis* as: " 1 a: the turning point for better or worse in an acute disease or fever b: a paroxysmal attack of pain, distress, or disordered function c: an emotionally significant event or radical change of status in a person's life 2: the decisive moment (as in a literary plot) 3 a: an unstable or crucial time or state of affairs in which a decisive change is impending; *esp* : one with the distinct possibility of a highly undesirable outcome b: a situation that has reached a critical phase." *Webster's Ninth New Collegiate Dictionary*, s.v. "crisis." Further definition to terms in this book have been extracted from this dictionary.

[5] Flannery and Everly, "Crisis Intervention," 119–25.

[6] Ibid., 120.

[7] Jill M. Hudson, *Congregational Trauma: Caring, Coping and Learning* (Herndon, Va.: Alban Institute, 1999), 16.

[8] Victor H. Mair, "Danger + Opportunity ≠ Crisis: How a Misunderstanding about Chinese Characters Has Led Many Astray," http://pinyin.info/chinese/crisis.html, last revised September 2009.

[9] Joseph Walsh and Jim Lantz, *Short-Term Existential Intervention in Clinical Practice* (Chicago: Lyceum Books, 2007), 5–6.

[10] George W. Bullard Jr., *Pursuing the Full Kingdom Potential of Your Congregation* (St. Louis: Lake Hickory Resources, 2005). One of the earliest to apply life-cycle thinking to congregational life was Martin Saarinen in *The Life Cycle of a Congregation* (Herndon, Va.: Alban Institute, 1986).

[11] In addition to George Bullard's book, mentioned in the previous note, here is a sampling of books that describe and respond to the crises of culture and purpose that churches face: Eddie Gibbs, *ChurchNext: Quantum Changes in How We Do Ministry* (Downers Grove, Ill.: InterVarsity Press, 2000) ; Darrell L. Guder, ed., *Missional Church: A Vision for the Sending of the Church in North America* (Grand Rapids, Mich.: William B. Eerdmans, 1998); Alan J. Roxburgh, *Introducing the Missional Church: What It Is, Why It Matters, How to Become One* (Grand Rapids, Mich.: Baker Books, 2009); Alan J. Roxburgh and Fred Romanuk, *The Missional Leader: Equipping Your Church to Reach a Changing World* (San Francisco: Jossey-Bass, 2006); Jim Herrington, Mike Bonem, and James H. Furr, *Leading Congregational Change* (San Francisco: Jossey-Bass, 2000); Robert Lewis and Wayne Cordeiro, *Culture Shift: Transforming*

Your Church from the Inside (San Francisco: Jossey-Bass, 2005); Brian D. McLaren, *The Church on the Other Side: Doing Ministry in the Postmodern Matrix* (Grand Rapids, Mich.: Zondervan, 2000); and Reggie McNeal, *The Present Future: Six Tough Questions for the Church* (San Francisco: Jossey-Bass, 2003).

[12] The crisis experience of Congregational United Church of Christ of Punta Gorda, Florida, is featured as a stand-alone story before chapter 8.

[13] The crisis experience of University Baptist Church of Waco, Texas, is featured as a stand-alone story before chapter 5.

[14] The crisis experience of New Life Church of Colorado Springs, Colorado, is featured as a stand-alone story before chapter 6.

[15] The crisis experience of Crosspointe Meadows Church of Novi, Michigan, is featured as a stand-alone story before chapter 7.

Chapter 3: Leadership, Management, and Crisis Care

[1] This quote is widely referenced on the internet. Drucker may well have said it first in a public address. For a close approximation of it in print, see Peter F. Drucker, *Management: Tasks, Responsibilities, Practices* (New York: Harper Business, 1993), 45. "Effectiveness is the foundation of success–efficiency is a minimum condition for survival *after* success has been achieved. Efficiency is concerned with doing things right. Effectiveness is doing the right things."

[2] Stephen R. Covey, *7 Habits of Highly Effective People* (New York: Simon & Schuster, 1989), 145–82.

[3] Ronald A. Heifetz and Marty Linsky, *Leadership on the Line: Staying Alive through the Dangers of Leading* (Boston: Harvard Business Press, 2002), 53, 65–67, 135, 165.

[4] My real-world appreciation for this grew as a result of conversations with leadership expert Gene Klann, whose distinguished twenty-five-year career in the Air Force and experience as a faculty member of the Center for Creative Leadership led to his appointment as associate professor of Command and Leadership at the U.S. Army Command and General Staff College in Leavenworth, Kansas. We discussed what the military does to promote these capacities, beginning with those in command who can, by exercising self-control and remaining poised, positive, and affirming under adverse conditions, greatly improve the chances of mission achievement and enhance the level of soldier resilience. Not surprisingly, one of the ways the military promotes soldier resilience is with training. They purposely push soldiers beyond their current levels of endurance, competence, and adaptability to prepare them for the stresses of armed conflict.

[5] Gene Klann, *Crisis Leadership: Using Military Lessons, Organizational Experience, and the Power of Influence to Lessen the Impact of Chaos on the People You Lead* (Greensboro, N.C.: Center for Creative Leadership, 2003), ix.

[6] For Giuliani's perspective on these leadership qualities, see Rudolph W. Giuliani, *Leadership* (New York: Hyperion, 2002).

[7] These three leaders and the crisis experiences of their congregations are featured among stand-alone stories that are located between chapters of the book.

Congregations in Focus: Wedgwood Baptist Church

[1] Wedgwood Baptist Church, "September 15, 1999," http://www.wedgwoodbc.org/content.cfm?id=2010.

[2] Sources for this story include a telephone interview with Pastor Al Meredith on November 11, 2010; various Web news sources; and Dan R. Crawford, *Night of Tragedy: Dawning of Light* (Colorado Springs: Shaw Books, 2000).

Chapter 4: When Crisis Strikes

[1] Rudyard Kipling, "If," in *Rewards and Fairies* (Charleston, S.C.: BiblioBazaar, 2007), 115.

[2] Laurence Barton, *Crisis Leadership Now* (New York: McGraw Hill, 2008), 294–95.

[3] Howard W. Stone, *Crisis Counseling* (Philadelphia: Fortress Press, 1976). This book remains a standard for pastoral intervention in crisis. Stone suggests an A, B, C strategy

for intervention: (a) Achieve personal contact with those in crisis–this is about establishing rapport through empathy and attending and listening skills; (b) boil down the problem to its essentials (each person experiences the crisis in their own way)–this involves paying attention to each person's physical condition, emotions, perceptions, and coping skills to get at the impact of the crisis on them; (c) cope actively with the problem–this has to do with helping people in crisis to identify and mobilize their coping resources and to supplement those as needed (32–48).

[4] Agostino Bono, "John Jay Study Reveals Extent of Abuse Problem," *Catholic News Service*, http://www.americancatholic.org/news/clergysexabuse/johnjaycns.asp.

[5] For more on this scandal, go to American Catholic, "The Catholic Church and Sexual Abuse by Priests Archive," http://www.americancatholic.org/news/clergysexabuse/default .asp.

[6] Harvard Business Press, *Crisis Management: Master the Skills to Prevent Disasters* (Boston: Harvard Business Press, 2004), 68–69.

[7] American College of Surgeons, *Advanced Trauma Life Support Program for Doctors*, 7th ed. (Chicago: American College of Surgeons, 2008).

[8] Gene Klann, *Crisis Leadership: Using Military Lessons, Organizational Experience, and the Power of Influence to Lessen the Impact of Chaos on the People You Lead* (Greensboro, N.C.: Center for Creative Leadership, 2003), 19.

[9] Edwin H. Friedman, *Generation to Generation: Family Process in Church and Synagogue* (New York: Guilford Press, 1985), 27, 208–10.

[10] Bill George, *7 Lessons for Leading in Crisis* (San Francisco: Jossey-Bass, 2009), 11.

[11] Barton, *Crisis Leadership Now*, 230–33.

[12] Philip L. Dubois, "Presidential Leadership in Time of Crisis," in *University Presidents as Moral Leaders*, ed. David G. Brown (Westport, Conn.: Praeger Publishers, 2006), 29–54. This address is also available online at http://www.uwyo.edu/news/shepard/PLD_book_chapter .htm.

[13] Associated Press, "Notre Dame President: School Responsible in Student's Death," *USA Today*, November 5, 2010, http://www.usatoday.com/sports/college/football/2010 -11-05-notre-dame-president-jenkins-sullivan-death_N.htm.

[14] Harvard Business Press, *Crisis Management*, 93–107.

Congregations in Focus: University Baptist Church

[1] Kyle Lake, *Understanding God's Will: How to Hack the Equation without Formulas* (Orlando, Fla.: Relevant Books, 2004); and Kyle Lake, *(RE)Understanding Prayer: A Fresh Approach to Conversation with God* (Orlando, Fla.: Relevant Books, 2005).

[2] Sources include telephone interviews with current teaching pastor Josh Carney and current community pastor Craig Nash on December 21, 2010; a telephone interview with former community pastor Ben Dudley on December 28, 2010; various internet news sources; and University Baptist Church's Web site, http://www.ubcwaco.org.

Chapter 5: Managing the Mess

[1] Harvard Business Press, *Crisis Management: Master the Skills to Prevent Disasters* (Boston: Harvard Business Press, 2004), 82–86.

[2] A modern English rendering of a line from Robert Burns's poem, "To a Mouse, on Turning Her Up in Her Nest with the Plough," in *The Norton Anthology of English Literature*, 3rd ed.,ed. M. H. Adams et al. (New York: W. W. Norton, 1974), 25, lines 39–40.

[3] M. Scott Peck, *The Road Less Traveled: A New Psychology of Love, Traditional Values and Spiritual Growth* (New York: Simon & Schuster, 1978), 15.

[4] Bill Hybels, *Axiom: Powerful Leadership Proverbs* (Grand Rapids, Mich.: Zondervan, 2008), 52.

[5] Brady Boyd, "Momentum and the Wind in Our Sails," April 14, 2009, http:// newlifeblogs.com/bradyboyd/2009/04/14/momentum-and-the-wind-in-our-sails/.

[6] Jill M. Hudson, *Congregational Trauma: Caring, Coping, and Learning* (Herndon, Va.: Alban Institute, 1998).

[7] Ibid., 129.

[8] Henri J. M. Nouwen, *The Wounded Healer* (New York: Doubleday, 1972).

[9] Ibid., xiv.

Congregations in Focus: New Life Church

[1] Sources include a telephone interview with Pastor Brady Boyd on December 8, 2010; a telephone interview with Ross Parsley on January 31, 2011; multiple Internet news sources related to both crises; and multiple postings of "Brady's Blog" on the church's Web site at http://www.newlifechurch.org. Boyd recounts the stories of crisis and celebrates what he calls "the miracle" that a church could survive two crises and thrive again in his recent book, *Fear No Evil: A Test of Faith, a Courageous Church, and an Unfailing God* (Grand Rapids, Mich.: Zondervan, 2011).

Chapter 6: Finding a New Normal

[1] Brady Boyd, "Momentum and the Wind in Our Sails," April 14, 2009, http://newlife-blogs.com/bradyboyd/2009/04/14/momentum-and-the-wind-in-our-sails/.

[2] Harvard Business Press, *Crisis Management: Master the Skills to Prevent Disasters* (Boston: Harvard Business Press, 2004), 82.

[3] Brady Boyd, "Big Mo," October 12, 2009, http://newlifeblogs.com/bradyboyd/2009/10/12/big-mo/.

[4] Lewis Smedes, *Forgive and Forget: Healing the Hurts We Don't Deserve* (San Francisco: Harper & Row, 1984), 136.

Congregations in Focus: Crosspointe Meadows Church

[1] For more about this resource, go to http://www.daveramsey.com/fpu/home.

[2] This story comes from a telephone interview with Pastor Danny Langley on October 20, 2010.

Chapter 7: Never Waste a Crisis

[1] Bill George, *7 Lessons for Leading in Crisis* (San Francisco: Jossey-Bass, 2009), 75.

[2] *Webster's Ninth New Collegiate Dictionary*, s.v. "crisis."

[3] Victor H. Mair, "Danger + Opportunity ≠ Crisis: How a Misunderstanding about Chinese Characters Has Led Many Astray," http://pinyin.info/chinese/crisis.html, last revised September 2009.

[4] W. Edwards Deming, *Out of the Crisis* (Cambridge, Mass.: Massachusetts Institute of Technology Center for Advanced Engineering Study, 1982).

[5] John Ortberg, "Don't Waste a Crisis," *Leadership Journal*, Winter 2011, 37–40.

[6] Ibid., 37.

[7] Edwin H. Friedman, *Generation to Generation: Family Process in Church and Synagogue* (New York: Guilford Press, 1985), 3, 27, 208–10.

[8] Harvard Business Press, *Crisis Management: Master the Skills to Prevent Disasters* (Boston: Harvard Business Press, 2004), 114–15.

[9] George W. Bullard Jr., *Pursuing the Full Kingdom Potential of Your Congregation* (St. Louis: Lake Hickory Resources, 2005), 76–78. He writes, "The longer Management drives and the longer Vision sleeps, the more likely the congregation will engage in activities that cause it to age and become more passive and less vital. The long-term result of this pattern is death."

[10] John C. Maxwell, *Failing Forward: Turning Mistakes into Stepping Stones for Success* (Nashville: Thomas Nelson Publishers, 2000).

[11] Peter M. Senge, *The Fifth Discipline: The Art & Practice of the Learning Organization* (New York: Currency Doubleday, 1994), 3.

Chapter 8: Getting in Front of Crisis

[1] San Diego Accident Lawyer, "Jury Awards $5 Million to Young Man Hurt on Church Ski Trip," October 1, 2010, http://www.personal-injury-attorney-in-san-diego.com/blog/archives/1175; and Todd Leskanic, "Jury Says Church Must Pay $4.75M," September 30, 2010, http://www2.tbo.com/news/metro/2010/sep/30/na-jury-says-church-must-pay-475m-ar-27429/.

[2] Bill Patterson, "A Crisis Management Plan: Are You Prepared?," http://www.disaster-resource.com/index.php?option=com_content&view=article&Itemid=1230&id=54:a-crisis-management-plan-are-you-prepared&catid=3.

[3] *The Church at Rock Creek Emergency Plan,* provided to the author as a digital resource by Sean McKean, Executive Pastor.

[4] Churchsafety.com, "Are We Prepared for Gun Violence at Church?" Churchsafety. com, cosponsored by Brotherhood Mutual Insurance and Christianity Today International, provides articles, assessment tools, and planning resources related to a full range of congregational risks.

[5] Laurence Barton, *Crisis Leadership Now* (New York: McGraw Hill, 2008), 241.

[6] Ian I. Mitroff, *Why Some Companies Emerge Stronger and Better from a Crisis: Seven Essential Lessons for Surviving Disaster* (New York: Amacom, 2005), 124.

[7] For example, the Center for Congregational Health, http://www.healthychurch .org; Healthy Congregations, http://www.healthycongregations.com; Leadership Network, http://www.leadnet.org; and Willow Creek Association, http://www.willowcreek.com.

[8] What follows is a somewhat arbitrary sampling of the vast and varied resources for defining and cultivating congregational health: George Bullard, *Pursuing the Full Kingdom Potential of Your Congregation* (St. Louis: Lake Hickory Resources, 2005); Darrell L. Guder, ed., *Missional Church: A Vision for the Sending of the Church in North America* (Grand Rapids, Mich.: William B. Eerdmans, 1998); Brian D. McLaren, *The Church on the Other Side: Doing Ministry in the Postmodern Matrix* (Grand Rapids, Mich.: Zondervan, 2000); Ronald W. Richardson, *Creating a Healthier Church* (Minneapolis: Fortress Press, 1996); Peter Steinke, *Healthy Congregations: A Systems Approach* (Herndon, Va.: Alban Institute, 2006); and Rick Warren, *The Purpose Driven Church* (Grand Rapids, Mich.: Zondervan, 1995).

[9] Bullard, *Full Kingdom Potential,* 72–73, 76.

Congregations in Focus: Sandy Run Baptist Church

[1] From personal interview with Paul Reid, pastor of Sandy Run Baptist Church, Hampton, S.C., on October 21, 2010.

Chapter 9: Faith and Crisis

[1] Used with permission of Dr. William Hull. It has found its way into worship services and onto walls around the world as a calligraphic reminder of the presence, purpose, and power of Christ.

[2] John Ortberg, "Don't Waste a Crisis," *Leadership Journal,* Winter 2011, 40.

[3] Consider, for example, Psalm 73:2–14; John 16:33; Romans 8:18–25; 1 Corinthians 10:13; Ephesians 6:12.

[4] Psalm 73:1, 15–28; Jeremiah 29:11; John 16:33; 1 Corinthians 10:13; Romans 5:1–5; Romans 8:28, 31–39.

[5] Psalm 23; Proverbs 3:5–6.

[6] 1 Thessalonians 4:13.

[7] 2 Timothy 1:12 (as translated into the words of the hymn, "I Know Whom I Have Believed," lyrics by Daniel Whittle, 1883).

[8] Joseph M. Martin, "Canticle of Hope," choral orchestration, lyrics by J. Paul Williams (Delaware Water Gap, Pa.: Shawnee Press), 1995.

[9] Chris Tomlin, Jesse Reeves, and Shawn Craig, "Mighty Is the Power of the Cross" (Brentwood, Tenn.: EMI Christian Music Publishing, 2004).

Chapter 10: Going the Distance

[1] American Psychological Association, "The Road to Resilience," http://www.apa.org/ helpcenter/road-resilience.aspx.

[2] Jerry L. Patterson, George A. Goens, and Diane E. Reed, *Resilient Leadership for Turbulent Times* (Lanham, Md.: Rowman & Littlefield, 2009), 8–11.

[3] You will have your own favorites to which you will turn, but some of those that have come to mean the most to me are: Joshua 1:1–9; Psalm 23; 27; 46; 121; Proverbs 3:5–6; Jeremiah 29:11–13; Matthew 28:20; John 16:33; Romans 5:1–5; 8:18–39 (and particularly vv. 28, 37–39); 1 Corinthians 10:13; 2 Corinthians 12:7–10; Ephesians 3:14–21; 6:10–18; Philippians 2:12–13; 4:6–7; 4:10–13; 4:19; James 1:2–4; Jude 24–25.

[4] APA, "The Road to Resilience," 4.

⁵ Patterson, *Resilient Leadership*, 9.

⁶ Paul Vitello, "Taking a Break from the Lord's Work," *New York Times*, August 1, 2010, http://www.nytimes.com/2010/08/02/nyregion/02burnout.html.

⁷ "Pastor Burnout Statistics," http://www.pastorburnout.com/pastor-burnout-statistics. html. A study on ministry burnout conducted by Austin Presbyterian Theological Seminary in partnership with the Favrot Fund surfaced similar concerns and vulnerabilities. For more, see Michael Jinkins, "Great Expectations, Sobering Realities: Findings from a New Study on Clergy Burnout," *Congregations*, May/June 2002.

⁸ Ruth Haley Barton, "A Steady Rhythm: The Not-So-Secret Key to Effective Ministry and Leadership," *Leadership*, January 1, 2007, http://www.christianitytoday.com/le/2007/winter/11.100.html.

⁹ Vitello, "Taking a Break from the Lord's Work."

¹⁰ Robert Hemfelt, Frank Minirth, and Paul Meier, *We Are Driven: The Compulsive Behaviors America Applauds* (Nashville: Thomas Nelson, 1991), 49–51; and Sheri S. Ferguson, "Clergy Compassion Fatigue," *Family Therapy Magazine*, March/April 2007, 17.

¹¹ Quoted in Mike Yaconelli, "I Don't Have Any Friends," *Leadership*, July 1, 1996, http://www.ctlibrary.com/le/1996/summer/6l3041.html.

¹² Bernard of Clairvaux, *On the Love of God; Classics of Faith and Devotion* (Portland, Ore.: Multnomah, 1983).

¹³ A reference to one of Saint Augustine's best known statements in *The Confessions, in Great Books of the Western World, Volume 18* (Chicago: Encyclopedia Britannica, 1952), Book I, 1.

¹⁴ Gordon MacDonald, "Pastor's Progress," *Leadership*, July 1, 1997, http://www.christianity today.com/le/1997/summer/7l3078.html.

¹⁵ Quoted in Richard J. Foster, *Celebration of Discipline*, rev. ed. (San Francisco: Harper & Row, 1988), 34.

¹⁶ John Ortberg, "Don't Waste a Crisis," *Leadership Journal*, Winter 2011, 40.

¹⁷ John M. Mulder, "In Pursuit of Excellence: Nurturing Protestant Pastoral Excellence," http://www.resourcingchristianity.org/research-article/in-pursuit-of-excellence-nurturing -protestant-pastoral-leadership.

¹⁸ M. Scott Peck, *The Road Less Traveled: A New Psychology of Love, Traditional Values and Spiritual Growth* (New York: Simon & Schuster, 1978), 15–18.

¹⁹ This popular quote can be found in the "Epistle Dedicatory to Arthur Bingham Walkley" in George Bernard Shaw, *Man and Superman* (CreateSpace, 2010), 21.

²⁰ See Hebrews 12:1–3, for example.

²¹ For example, see Genesis 12:1–3; Hebrews 11:8.

Resources for Crisis Leadership

Leadership

Jim Collins, *Good to Great and the Social Sectors* (Boulder: Jim Collins, 2005).

Peter F. Drucker, *Managing the Non-Profit Organization: Principles and Practices* (New York: HarperBusiness, 1990).

Ronald A. Heifetz and Marty Linsky, *Leadership on the Line: Staying Alive through the Dangers of Leading* (Boston: Harvard Business Press, 2002).

John P. Kotter, *Leading Change* (Boston: Harvard Business Press, 1996).

Peter M. Senge, *The Fifth Discipline: The Art & Practice of the Learning Organization* (New York: Currency Doubleday, 1994).

Congregational Leadership

George Bullard, *Pursuing the Full Kingdom Potential of Your Congregation* (St. Louis: Lake Hickory Resources, 2005).

The Center for Congregational Health, http://www.healthychurch.org.

Edwin H. Friedman, *Generation to Generation: Family Process in Church and Synagogue* (New York: Guilford Press, 1985).

Adam Hamilton, *Leading Beyond the Walls: Developing Congregations with a Heart for the Unchurched* (Nashville: Abingdon, 2002).

Healthy Congregations, http://www.healthycongregations.com.

Jim Herrington, Mike Bonem, and James H. Furr, *Leading Congregational Change* (San Francisco: Jossey-Bass, 2000).

Bill Hybels, *Axiom: Powerful Leadership Proverbs* (Grand Rapids, Mich.: Zondervan, 2008).

Dan Kimball, *The Emerging Church: Vintage Christianity for New Generations* (Grand Rapids, Mich.: Zondervan, 2003).

Leadership Network, http://www.leadnet.org.

Robert Lewis and Wayne Cordeiro, *Culture Shift: Transforming Your Church from the Inside* (San Francisco: Jossey-Bass, 2005).

Alan J. Roxburgh and Fred Romanuk, *The Missional Leader: Equipping Your Church to Reach a Changing World* (San Francisco: Jossey-Bass, 2006).

Willow Creek Association, http://www.willowcreek.com.

Healthy Leaders

American Psychological Association, "The Road to Resilience," http://www.apa .org/helpcenter/road-resilience.aspx.

Stephen R. Covey, *7 Habits of Highly Effective People* (New York: Simon & Schuster, 1989).

Richard J. Foster, *Celebration of Discipline*, rev. ed. (San Francisco: Harper & Row, 1988).

Bill George and Peter Sims, *True North: Discover Your Authentic Leadership* (San Francisco: John Wiley & Sons, 2007).

Anne Jackson, *Mad Church Disease: Overcoming the Burnout Epidemic* (Grand Rapids, Mich.: Zondervan, 2009).

John C. Maxwell, *Failing Forward: Turning Mistakes into Stepping Stones for Success* (Nashville: Thomas Nelson Publishers, 2000).

Jerry L. Patterson, George A. Goens, and Diane E. Reed, *Resilient Leadership for Turbulent Times* (Lanham, Md.: Rowman & Littlefield, 2009).

M. Scott Peck, *The Road Less Traveled: A New Psychology of Love, Traditional Values and Spiritual Growth* (New York: Simon & Schuster, 1978).

Michael Todd Wilson and Brad Hoffman, *Preventing Ministry Failure* (Downer's Grove, Ill.: InterVarsity Press, 2007).

Healthy Congregations

Diana Butler Bass, *The Practicing Congregation* (Herndon, Va.: Alban Institute, 2004).

George W. Bullard Jr., *Pursuing the Full Kingdom Potential of Your Congregation* (St. Louis: Lake Hickory Resources, 2005).

Darrell L. Guder, ed., *Missional Church: A Vision for the Sending of the Church in North America* (Grand Rapids, Mich.: William B. Eerdmans, 1998).

Brian D. McLaren, *The Church on the Other Side: Doing Ministry in the Postmodern Matrix* (Grand Rapids, Mich.: Zondervan, 2000).

Reggie McNeal, *The Present Future: Six Tough Questions for the Church* (San Francisco: Jossey-Bass, 2003).

Ronald W. Richardson, *Creating a Healthier Church* (Minneapolis: Fortress Press, 1996).

Alan J. Roxburgh, *Introducing the Missional Church: What It Is, Why It Matters, How to Become One* (Grand Rapids, Mich.: Baker Books, 2009).

Peter Scazzero and Warren Bird, *The Emotionally Healthy Church: A Strategy for Discipleship That Actually Changes Lives* (Grand Rapids, Mich.: Zondervan, 2010).

Peter Steinke, *Healthy Congregations: A Systems Approach* (Herndon, Va.: Alban Institute, 2006).

Rick Warren, *The Purpose Driven Church* (Grand Rapids, Mich.: Zondervan, 1995).

Crisis Leadership and Management

Laurence Barton, *Crisis Leadership Now* (New York: McGraw Hill, 2008).

Steven Fink, *Crisis Management: Planning for the Inevitable*, Backinprint.com (Lincoln, Nebr.: iUniverse, 2007).

Bill George, *7 Lessons for Leading in Crisis* (San Francisco: Jossey-Bass, 2009).

Rudolph W. Giuliani, *Leadership* (New York: Hyperion, 2002).

Harvard Business Press, *Crisis Management: Master the Skills to Prevent Disasters* (Boston: Harvard Business Press, 2004).

Harvard Business Press, *Leading Through a Crisis* (Boston: Harvard Business Press, 2009).

Gene Klann, *Crisis Leadership: Using Military Lessons, Organizational Experience, and the Power of Influence to Lessen the Impact of Chaos on the People You Lead*

(Greensboro, N.C.: Center for Creative Leadership, 2003).

Ian I. Mitroff, *Why Some Companies Emerge Stronger and Better from a Crisis: Seven Essential Lessons for Surviving Disaster* (New York: Amacom, 2005).

Donald T. Phillips, *Lincoln on Leadership: Executive Strategies for Tough Times* (New York: Warner Books, 1992).

Crisis Leadership for Congregations

Jill M. Hudson, *Congregational Trauma: Caring, Coping and Learning* (Herndon, Va.: Alban Institute, 1998).

Henri J. M. Nouwen, *The Wounded Healer* (New York: Doubleday, 1972).

Peter L. Steinke, *Congregational Leadership in Anxious Times: Being Calm and Courageous No Matter What* (Herndon, Va.: Alban Institute, 2006).

Howard W. Stone, *Crisis Counseling* (Philadelphia: Fortress Press, 1976).

Resources for Dealing with Specific Critical Issues

Crisis- and Risk-Related Support Organizations

Brotherhood Mutual Insurance Company, http://www.brotherhoodmutual.com.
Brotherhood Mutual has its own extensive library of information related to a broad range of risk management topics. Though there is some overlap of information between this site and the Churchsafety.com site, there are additional resources here, including articles, guidebooks, checklists, safety training, legal assistance, and a wide variety of risk management forms.

Churchcentral.com, http://www.churchcentral.com.
Created by Thom Rainer, now CEO of LifeWay Resources, and Tom Harper, ChurchCentral president, this site is dedicated to building healthy churches. It provides insight and advice from well-known authors and researchers on a variety of topics, including risk and crisis management.

Churchsafety.com, http://www.churchsafety.com.
Christianity Today International and Brotherhood Mutual Insurance Company have joined forces to provide this outstanding Web site with expert advice and risk management information for congregations on a broad range of topics. Extremely easy to navigate, the site provides free articles and online risk assessments, premium downloads for planning and discussion, and an interactive question and answer feature with an archive of expert responses to questions people have asked in the past.

Directions Inc., http://GregoryLHunt.com.
Directions Inc. is the nonprofit organization through which I serve people as they lead their organizations, relationships, and lives. Resourcing congregations is integral to our nonprofit mission.

The International Critical Incident Stress Foundation, http://www.icisf.org.
ICISF provides leadership, education, training, consultation, and support services in crisis intervention and disaster behavior health services to

emergency response professionals, other organizations, and communities worldwide. They maintain a database of trained teams. Their Web site includes an extensive list of articles and resources.

The National Association of Church Business Administration, http://www.nacba .net.

The NACBA is an interdenominational, professional, Christian organization which exists to serve the Church by advancing professional excellence in individuals serving Christ through administration in local churches. They provide conferences, events, resources, education, and networking on a wide range of topics, including risk management.

Developing a Risk Management Plan

Ron Aguiar, *Keeping Your Church Safe* (Camarillo, Calif.: Xulon Press, 2009).

Brotherhoodmutual.com, "Creating a Risk Management Plan."

Brotherhoodmutual.com, "Developing a Risk Management Mindset."

Brotherhoodmutual.com, "How to Spot Potential Risks."

Brotherhoodmutual.com, "Key Areas of Potential Risk for Churches."

Brotherhoodmutual.com, "Safety 101."

Brotherhoodmutual.com, "Six Steps to Reducing Risk."

James F. Cobble Jr. and Richard R. Hammar, *Risk Management Handbook for Churches and Schools* (Carol Stream, Ill.: Your Church Resources/Christianity Today, 2007).

Wayne Garst, *Checklist for a Church Emergency Management Plan,* n.d., http://www .brethren.org/bdm/files/checklist_for_a_church_emergency_management _plan.pdf.

GuideOne Center for Risk Management, *The Missing Ministry: Safety, Risk Management, and Protecting Your Church* (Loveland, Colo.: Group Publishing, 2008).

Preparing Your Church for Any Emergency: Powerful Practices That Keep People Safe (Carol Stream, Ill.: Christianity Today, 2006).

Risk Prevention & Crisis Management Manual (Silver Spring, Md.: Adventist Risk Management, 2005).

Lisa Schuler, *A Risk Management Plan* (Dallas: NACBA, 2008).

Accidents and Emergencies

Brotherhoodmutual.com, "Accident Medical Emergency Guidelines."

Brotherhoodmutual.com, "Managing High Risk Activities."

Churchsafety.com, "Be Prepared for Nursery Accidents and Injuries."

Churchsafety.com, "Can Our Church Handle a Medical Emergency?"

Churchsafety.com, "Do We Keep Our Property Safe?"

Churchsafety.com, "International Safety Overseas."

Churchsafety.com, "Is Our Facility Safe from Risk of Fire?"

Churchsafety.com, "Is Your Playground Safe?"

Churchsafety.com, "Keeping Recreational Facilities Safe."

Churchsafety.com, "Planning for Emergency Evacuations."

Churchsafety.com, "Planning Safe Mission Trips."

Churchsafety.com, "Preparing Your Church for Any Emergency."

Churchsafety.com, "Transportation Safety for Your Church."
Churchsafety.com, "Your Guide to a Safe Church Day Care."

Business Continuity

Brotherhoodmutual.com, "Cyber Security: Protecting Your Computer from Malicious Software."
Brotherhoodmutual.com, "Cyber Security: Shield Church Information from Online Thieves."
Brotherhoodmutual.com, "Disaster Recovery Planning: Ministry Continuity Checklist."
Brotherhoodmutual.com, "Documents and Records: What You Should Know."
Brotherhoodmutual.com, "Ministry Continuity Worksheet."
Brotherhoodmutual.com, "Protecting Your Equipment Investment."
Churchsafety.com, "Church Computer Safety."
Churchsafety.com, "Protecting Electronic Data."
Nick B. Nicholaou, "Protecting IT from Disasters," http://www.christianitytoday.com.

Conflict and Crisis

David Brubaker, *Promise and Peril: Understanding and Managing Change and Conflict in Congregations* (Herndon, Va.: Alban Institute, 2009).
George Bullard, *Every Congregation Needs a Little Conflict*, TCP Leadership Series (St. Louis: Chalice Press, 2008).
George Bullard, "Leaving, Staying, and Becoming Well Following a Lose/Leave Conflict in a Congregation," *NACBA Ledger*, Spring 2011, 13–16.
David B. Lott, ed., *Conflict Management in Congregations* (Herndon, Va.: Alban Institute, 2001).
Larry L. McSwain, "Mending the Tears of Church Conflict," *NACBA Ledger*, Spring 2011, 6–11.

Crime and Violence

Brotherhoodmutual.com, "Arson-Proof Your Church."
Brotherhoodmutual.com, "Eleven Ways to Avoid Arson."
Brotherhoodmutual.com, "Preparing for the Unthinkable: Violence in the Church."
Brotherhoodmutual.com, "Surviving a Violent Attack at Church."
Brotherhoodmutual.com, "Violence in the Church Emergency Checklist."
Churchsafety.com, "Are We Prepared for Gun Violence at Church?"
Churchsafety.com, "Dealing with Dangerous People."
Churchsafety.com, "Do We Prevent Crime at Our Church?"
Churchsafety.com, "Guard Against Copper Thieves."
Churchsafety.com, "Is Our Church Secure from Crime and Violence?"
Churchsafety.com, "Protecting Your Church from Crime and Violence."

Disasters

Brotherhoodmutual.com, "Developing a Disaster Plan."
Brotherhoodmutual.com, "Recovering from the Storm."

Brotherhoodmutual.com, "Sending Disaster Relief Teams."
Churchsafety.com, "Communicating in a Crisis."
Churchsafety.com, "Is Our Church Prepared for a Disaster?"
Churchsafety.com, "Serving as a Disaster Relief Team."
Churchsafety.com, "Simple Ways to Deal with Disaster."
Churchsafety.com, "When Disaster Strikes."
North American Mission Board, "Church Preparedness for Disaster," http://www.churchdisasterhelp.org/files/manuals/Church%20Preparedness%20Manual.pdf.

Grief

Wayne E. Oates, *Grief, Transition, and Loss: A Pastor's Practical Guide* (Minneapolis: Augsburg, 1997).
David K. Switzer, *Pastoral Care Emergencies* (Minneapolis: Augsburg, 2000).
Granger E. Westberg, *Good Grief* (Philadelphia: Fortress Press, 1971).

Financial Crises

Brotherhoodmutual.com, "Protect Your Finances with Internal Cash Controls."
Churchsafety.com, "Are We Growing Generous Givers?"
Churchsafety.com, "Do We Safely Handle Our Money?"
Churchsafety.com, "How Secure Is Your Church's Current System?"
Churchsafety.com, "Internal Controls for Church Finances."
Churchsafety.com, "Is Our Money Safe?"
Keith Hamilton, "Keys to Solving Your Church's Financial Crisis," http://www.lifeway.com.
Vern Hargrave, "Ten Ingredients of Effective Fraud Prevention," *NACBA Ledger*, Spring 2011, 46–52.

Legal Concerns

Brotherhoodmutual.com, "Avoiding Copyright-Related Lawsuits."
Brotherhoodmutual.com, "Top 10 Legal Issues."
Churchsafety.com, "Are We Ready for a Sexual Misconduct Allegation?"
Churchsafety.com, "Avoiding Church Lawsuits."
Churchsafety.com, "Copyright Law: What Every Church Must Know."
Churchsafety.com, "Do You Follow the Fair Labor Standards Act?"
Churchsafety.com, "Lay Counseling Safety."
Churchsafety.com, "Preventing Top Tax Pitfalls."
Churchsafety.com, "Sexual Harassment in Your Church."
Churchsafety.com, "Understanding Wage and Hour Laws."

Misconduct

Candace R. Benyei, *Understanding Clergy Misconduct in Religious Systems: Scapegoating, Family Secrets, and the Abuse of Power* (Binghamton, N.Y.: Haworth Press, 1998).
Brotherhoodmutual.com, "Addressing Online Pornography."
Brotherhoodmutual.com, "Reducing the Risk of Misconduct in Your Ministry."
Brotherhoodmutual.com, "Sex Offenders: Should They Be Allowed in Church?"

Brotherhoodmutual.com, "Take Steps to Prevent Child Abuse."
Churchsafety.com, "Are We Protecting Our Youth Ministry?"
Churchsafety.com, "Are We Ready for a Sexual Misconduct Allegation?"
Churchsafety.com, "Are We Screening Our Teen Volunteers?"
Churchsafety.com, "How Does Our Ministry Maintain Emotional Safety?"
Churchsafety.com, "Lay Counseling Safety."
Churchsafety.com, "Screening Underage Workers."
Churchsafety.com, "Sexual Harassment in Your Church."
Churchsafety.com, "What Counseling Precautions Are We Taking?"
Beth Ann Gaede, ed., *When a Congregation Is Betrayed: Responding to Clergy Misconduct* (Herndon, Va.: Alban Institute, 2006).
Nancy Myer Hopkins and Mark Laaser, eds., *Restoring the Soul of a Church: Healing Congregations Wounded by Clergy Sexual Misconduct* (Collegeville, Minn.: Liturgical Press, 1995).
Karen McClintock, *Preventing Sexual Abuse in Congregations: A Resource for Leaders* (Herndon, Va.: Alban Institute, 2004).

Personnel Crises

Churchsafety.com, "Can You Handle a Firing?"
Churchsafety.com, "Do We Know How to Create a Severance Agreement?"
Churchsafety.com, "How Compliant Are Our Employment Practices?"
Churchsafety.com, "Understanding Wage and Hour Laws."

Sudden Death

Jill M. Hudson, *Congregational Trauma: Caring, Coping and Learning* (Herndon, Va.: Alban Institute, 1998).

Trauma

George S. Everly Jr., "'Pastoral Crisis Intervention': Toward a Definition," *International Journal of Emergency Mental Health* 2(2) (2000): 69–71.
George S. Everly Jr. and Jeffrey T. Mitchell, "A Primer on Critical Incident Stress Management," http://www.icisf.org.
Raymond B. Flannery Jr., "Psychological Trauma and Posttraumatic Stress Disorder: A Review," *International Journal of Emergency Mental Health* 2(2) (2000): 77–82.
Raymond B. Flannery Jr. and George S. Everly Jr., "Crisis Intervention: A Review," *International Journal of Emergency Mental Health* 2(2) (2000): 119–25.
Andrew Weaver, Laura T. Flannelly, and John D. Preston, *Counseling Survivors of Traumatic Events: A Handbook for Pastors and Other Helping Professionals* (Nashville: Abingdon, 2003).